Praise for Cy Charney
and *The Portable Mentor*

"... perfect ... smart advice for everybody from a great mentor — and all between two covers!"
— PETER URS BENDER, BESTSELLING AUTHOR OF *SECRETS OF POWER MARKETING*, *LEADERSHIP FROM WITHIN*, AND *SECRETS OF POWER PRESENTATIONS*

"It's about time! Finally someone has written a well-thought-out, readable, and organized manual on mentoring. I was up half the night reading the manual and then spent the other half thinking about all the great ideas I got from it."
— CLAUDE "THE MENTOR" DIAMOND, AUTHOR OF *MENTORING TO MILLIONS*

"In this fast-paced, learn-on-the-run world, everyone needs a smart mentor, but they're not always around when you need one. *The Portable Mentor* provides cutting-edge wisdom on a huge array of subjects, each critical to high performance and ongoing success. Buy two — one for home and one for work!"
— CHIP R. BELL, AUTHOR OF *MANAGERS AS MENTORS*

"Charney has created a learning encyclopedia filled with practical advice for front-line workers. The book itself is the mentor — dispensing information and wisdom to all readers."

— REY CARR, PRESIDENT OF PEER RESOURCES

"Wow! I've never seen a book that is so full of practical common-sense ideas. And its layout makes it so easy to access information quickly. A must-have for all staff."

— PETER ZARRY, DIRECTOR, EXECUTIVE PROGRAMS, SCHULICH SCHOOL OF BUSINESS, YORK UNIVERISTY

For more information on Cy Charney and
his organization, see his web page at
http://home.istar.ca/~charney/
or email Cy at: charney@istar.ca

The Portable Mentor

Your Complete Guide to Getting Ahead in the Workplace

Cy Charney

Published in 2000 by Stoddart Publishing Co. Limited
34 Lesmill Road, Toronto, Canada M3B 2T6

Distributed by:
General Distribution Services Ltd.
325 Humber College Blvd., Toronto, Canada M9W 7C3
Tel. (416) 213-1919   Fax (416) 213-1917
Email cservice@genpub.com

04 03 02 01 00   1 2 3 4 5

Canadian Cataloguing in Publication Data

Charney, Cyril
The portable mentor: your complete guide to
getting ahead in the workplace

ISBN 0-7737-6069-5

1. Success in business — Handbooks, manuals, etc.
2. Mentoring in business — Handbooks, manual, etc.
I. Title.

HF5386.C42 2000   650.1   C99-932673-2

Cover Design: Bill Douglas @ The Bang
Text Design: Tannice Goddard

THE CANADA COUNCIL | LE CONSEIL DES ARTS
FOR THE ARTS | DU CANADA
SINCE 1957 | DEPUIS 1957

*We acknowledge for their financial support of our
publishing program the Canada Council, the Ontario Arts
Council, and the Government of Canada through the
Book Publishing Industry Development Program (BPIDP).*

Printed and bound in Canada

To my three unique, wonderful,
and special children:

Daneal, whose zest for life and independence
amaze me,
Thalia, whose single-mindedness and
dedication inspire me, and
Davin, whose passion and soul uplift me.

Contents

Preface

It takes only one match to light a forest fire.

*F*uturists believe that the intellectual capital of an organization will be its most important competitive weapon in the next century. They're wrong. It already is. Trained, knowledgeable people are the key ingredients for success. Conventional approaches to learning, such as classroom training, are giving way to alternative learning approaches such as mentoring and peer learning. Research shows conclusively that when people take responsibility for their own learning, retention is higher, application increases, and costs are lower. "Ownership" is typically not part of conventional training programs.

An effective mentoring program matches the needs and expectations of a protegé with the expertise of a mentor. Both require training, encouragement, incentives, and tools. *The Portable Mentor* is designed to be one of those tools of development. It focuses on non-technical skills. Since no mentor has answers to all the questions that protegés might ask, I decided to help by providing a quick reference guide with thousands of ideas. This book is designed to help mentors find answers for their protegés. It will also help protegés to be more self-sufficient by giving them a tool to assist them in finding their own solutions. In this way protegés can gradually wean themselves from their mentors — the ultimate measure of success.

The Portable Mentor is a collection of conventional wisdom that I, as a mentor to many people over the last quarter century, have been asked to provide. It will enable you to take more responsibility for your own growth and career — and success.

ACKNOWLEDGEMENTS

No one person can put together a book with so many ideas. So, as before, I have been fortunate to have had guidance and advice from people with whom I work. Those who have made a significant contribution to the book include Chips Klein, President, Chipco Canada Inc., Thornhill, ON; Heather Taylor, HR Consultant, Toronto, ON; Shelly Zaidman-Averbuch, Doctor of Naturopathic Medicine, Thornhill, ON; Thalia Charney; Dianne Conrad, Program Manager, Certificate in Adult and Continuing Education, University of Alberta, Calgary, AB; Rhona Charney, Psychotherapist, Bellwood Health Care, Scarborough, ON; David Wright, Manager, Corporate Learning, Canada Trust, Toronto, ON; Bruce McAlpine, Partner, The Keith Bagg Group, Toronto, ON.

Absenteeism

I finally got my head together, when my body fell apart!

ANONYMOUS

Absenteeism costs everyone. It increases your organization's costs since temporary staff might need to be hired or your colleagues might need to work overtime. It reduces your customer service, since fill-in workers are less effective. And it aggravates fellow employees, who are often called upon to pick up the slack. A great attendance record will speak volumes to your employer about your commitment to the organization.

Make every effort to get to work. Your absence disrupts the services you provide and causes stress for your peers, who will need to cover for you.

1. There are times when you should not go to work. These include the times when
   - you are sick with something that may infect other people, thereby exacerbating the problem;
   - your state of health requires that you be under medication, which could cause an accident.

2. If you need to be away, call in early so that your associates can deal with the shortage as quickly as possible.

3. Take care of your health, and you will miss work much less often. Here are some tips that will contribute to your well-being:

- Think wellness. Be positive. Be optimistic. Your mind will enhance your immunity to illness.
- Exercise regularly. Don't do things you hate to do — they will be short-lived. Do things you enjoy, such as skating, walking around a mall — anything that improves your heart rate. Then, as you get fit, increase the rate and frequency of exercising without putting pressure on yourself. Make exercise your choice — walk up stairs, walk to the store. You'll feel better mentally and physically.
- Drink lots of water. Water will purify the body and help you feel less inclined to eat.
- Have fun. Plan to do things that make you laugh and smile. These feelings wipe away the stress normally associated with the daily routines we experience at work.
- Take frequent stretch breaks. At tea/coffee breaks and at lunch, stretch your body. You will feel increased energy.
- Improve your nutrition intake. People say you are what you eat. While you never want to give up those foods that give you pleasure, you should think about cutting down on red meats and fatty foods. Eat more fruit and vegetables. You will feel and look better as a result. Also, eat more frequently, so you don't have that starving feeling that might cause you to binge.

Accident Prevention

*P*reventing accidents is everybody's job. These prevention activities have a huge payback, both financially and in terms of morale.

1. Be extra cautious when using toxic substances. If allowed to enter the body, they can cause damage to your nervous system, bones, or reproductive organs. They can be inhaled as dust, fumes, mists, vapours, or gases.

Toxic substances can enter your body if you
- eat in a dusty area;
- fail to wash your hands before eating;
- lick your lips while working with toxic chemicals or in a dusty area;
- forget to cover your food in a dusty area.

2. Reduce your risk of toxic poisoning by
- encouraging the replacement of toxic chemicals with more benign products;
- protecting yourself with goggles, gloves, and adequate overalls;
- ensuring that the process takes place in an enclosed area;
- improving ventilation;
- having written procedures for handling dangerous chemicals;

- rotating tasks so that your exposure is more limited;
- showering before going home each day;
- eating as far away from the hazardous areas as possible;
- being trained in what substances can harm you, how to handle chemicals safely, how to get rid of chemical waste safely, appropriate clothing and its care, and how to deal with an emergency;
- reporting concerns such as spills, unusual odours, and leaks.

3. Take care of your hearing. Ill effects are non-reversible. Ensure that
- machines are maintained regularly, so they are less noisy;
- sound-absorbing materials are used where possible;
- noisy machines are enclosed;
- noise is directed away from employees;
- you wear appropriate hearing-protection equipment at all times.

4. Improve the ergonomics of your workplace. Ergonomics is the science of making work fit individuals, to prevent injuries such as
- back sprains;
- pain in the shoulders, arms, or neck;
- eye strain;
- repetitive sprains.

5. Typical problems that can be addressed by ergonomic solutions include:
- constant reaching;
- frequent bending;
- a need to stand or sit in one place for prolonged periods of time;
- a need to use tools that require a repetitive motion to work.

6. Take action to prevent a problem by
   - asking for help to change the way you work;
   - suggesting improvements;
   - being particularly careful when lifting heavy objects;
   - not standing or sitting in one place for too long — stretch often;
   - making adjustments to the work station to help you;
   - discussing your concerns with the supervisor or members of your Health and Safety committee, or both.

7. Back strains are the most common workplace injury. Avoid them by
   - following workplace practices;
   - shifting your body frequently, so as to avoid rigidity;
   - using equipment the way it was designed to be used;
   - asking for help if you anticipate a problem;
   - stretching frequently;
   - exercising your back muscles;
   - wearing shoes with low heels and non-skid soles.

8. If you need to move heavy objects:
   - Plan the move before you start.
   - Anticipate the weight and figure out the easiest way of moving the object.
   - Get help, if necessary.
   - Stand with your feet spread shoulder-width apart.
   - Crouch down to get a firm grip on the object.
   - Keep the item close to your body as if you were hugging it.
   - Use your leg muscles to left the item. Keep your back straight.
   - Make sure you can see where you are going.
   - Move slowly but surely.
   - Avoid twisting. Turn with your feet, not your waist.

Anger

Did you ever notice how difficult it is to argue with someone who is not obsessed about being right?

WAYNE W. DYER

Anger is a natural part of life. Like conflict, anger can be positive if it mobilizes you to overcome obstacles. But if it is focused on people, it can be destructive. These ideas will help you reduce the negative effects of anger.

YOUR OWN

1.
- Acknowledge your anger.
- Identify the source of your anger. Is this person or event the real source, or just a trigger for unresolved, and perhaps unrelated, anger?
- Act, don't react. Focus on events, actions, and things, not on the person.
- If you feel "out of control," take a deep breath, count to ten, and try to respond as calmly as possible. If this is difficult, leave the situation until you feel ready to deal with it calmly and rationally. Talk to a third person first, if necessary.

- If you are documenting your concerns and others will read your notes, don't send the first draft. Wait twenty-four hours to review your tone and choice of language. If possible, have a trusted and objective colleague edit your work.

FROM OTHERS

2.
- Listen while the person vents his anger.
- Mirror her behaviour by adopting a similar position. Sit if she is seated, stand if she is standing.
- Allow him to finish, so he has everything off his chest.
- Show empathy. Acknowledge her right to be angry.
- Validate his position. Confirm your agreement with him and/or an understanding of the issues.
- Don't use language that might trigger further anger.
- Maintain a calm, quiet posture and speak in a calm tone (measured volume and pace).
- Help the person deal with the problem so that it does not recur.
- Ask the person to document more complex problems. Set up a time to review concerns.

Assertiveness

*To know how to refuse is as important
as to know how to consent.*

BALTASSAR GRACIAN

*A*ssertiveness is not aggressiveness. It is about standing up for yourself, not looking for a fight. Assertive people express their needs through honest, unbiased, and non-confrontational communication.

1. Improve your self-esteem by taking care of your needs. When you act assertively you feel good about yourself, because you react appropriately to situations and deal with your frustrations.

2. Learn to recognize the difference between assertiveness and aggression. Don't be aggressive. Focus on the problem rather than on the person who is causing you frustration.

3. Learn to say no without feeling guilty. You are entitled to your own feelings and needs.

4. You may find that your heart is pounding and your hands are shaking, but don't lose control. Assertiveness will get easier.

5. Stand tall, with shoulders relaxed, as you face your "opponent." Keep your gaze open and direct, but avoid a challenging, fixed stare.

6. Speak firmly, clearly, and in a moderate tone. The more sure your voice sounds, the more confident you will feel.

7. Describe the immediate situation that is causing you concern (for example, "This report is missing its table of contents").

8. Make known your feelings (for example, "I am really upset that the report was sent out without an important section").

9. Show with your voice and your body the importance of having your concerns addressed.
- Speak with a firm voice.
- Express your needs clearly and slowly.
- Lean forward.
- Maintain eye contact.

10. Make "I" statements. This is the true essence of assertive behaviour. It makes your wishes and expectations clear without putting the other person on the defensive. Use, for example, the phrases "I want," "I feel," "I would like."

11. Don't get tangled up in side issues as you are making your point. If the conversation is getting off-track, you might say, "I understand how you feel, but I'd like to resolve this issue first."

12. If you feel that the other person is trying to manipulate or sidetrack you, use the broken-record technique. Repeat your message as many times as necessary. For example, say, "We can talk about that another time. Right now, we are talking about —."

13. Be very clear about what you want — don't generalize. Saying "It is important that reports are done by the sixth of the month" is better than "All my work needs to be done quickly."

14. Describe the consequences of not achieving the goal for both of you.

15. If you have to refuse a request, don't begin with an apology. You do not have to say you're sorry if you're not. Say no politely but firmly, and keep your explanation short and clear. Long explanations confuse the issue.

16. If your discussion is going nowhere, review the process. Say, for example, "I feel we are going around in circles. This frustrates me. What am I doing wrong? I can't seem to get my point across."

17. Be firm in expressing your own case, but do not ignore the other person's point of view. Be ready to listen and consider other positions. Welcome a chance to agree on any reasonable points, but hold your ground on issues that you still find unacceptable.

18. When all else fails, look for a compromise. You may say, "Let's agree to disagree," and then move on, avoiding the person or the issue to the best of your ability.

ASSERTIVENESS
SELF-TEST

Do you need to improve your assertiveness? Answer yes or no to the following questions.

	YES	NO
I am not the final judge of whether my behaviour offends others.		
I feel I have to apologize if I don't have the answer to a question right away.		
I always say I'm sorry when I disagree with other people.		
If I change my mind about something, I feel guilty.		
I say yes every time someone asks for help.		
Making mistakes makes me feel guilty, even when I know how to fix them.		
I don't feel I can ask others to change the way they behave towards me.		
I am embarrassed when I don't understand other people.		
I don't feel I have the right to defer less important tasks.		
I can't say no to things people ask me to do, even if I can't or don't want to do them.		
I am afraid to walk away when someone starts arguing with me.		
My opinion doesn't count, especially if I don't agree with the majority.		
I don't dare ask questions when someone is giving me instructions.		

- If you have answered yes to 8 to 11 statements, you should make a major effort to be more assertive.
- If you have answered yes to 4 to 7 statements, your assertiveness could be improved.
- If you have answered yes to 0 to 3 statements, you have a good sense of your self-worth.

Attitude Survey

People's attitudes directly affect their workplace effectiveness. If an organization can improve its workers' level of morale, it will probably also realize improved productivity and customer satisfaction.

Frequent staff turnover and absenteeism are strong indicators of an unhappy workforce. The best way to find out what is causing low morale is to take an attitude survey. This will enable your organization to collect measurable data and determine specific reasons for discontent.

If your organization or department is carrying out an attitude survey, you can assist in the improvement of workplace morale with the following positive responses.

BEFORE THE SURVEY

1. Attend any information meetings with a positive attitude. However, satisfy yourself that the survey is legitimate, and that it is being conducted professionally and for purposes that will benefit staff. To do so, you will want to ask

- what steps are being taken to ensure the anonymity of the participants;
- what assurances and safeguards there are that all the information will be fed back to the participants;

- how long it will take for the feedback to be made available;
- what steps will be taken to ensure that the data will be acted upon;
- whether front-line staff will be able to have any input into the questions that will be used in the survey.

DURING THE SURVEY

2.
- Answer all questions frankly.
- Do not write your name anywhere on the questionnaire if anonymity is important to you.

DURING THE FEEDBACK SESSION

3.
- Ask for a copy of the results so you can study them in more detail at your leisure. If the complete survey is not available for everyone, ask if you can access it somewhere in the organization.
- Help to keep the meeting positive. Do not try to embarrass anyone through your questions. Focus more on next steps and new action plans than on finger-pointing.
- Volunteer to take care of some actions. Focus on items over which you have control. This will encourage others to get involved too; more of the issues will be dealt with if they are not all left to your manager.

AFTER THE SURVEY

4.
- Keep the interest in the survey going by referring to it and the action plans that were developed previously.

Benchmarking

Benchmarking is the continuous process of measuring products, services, and practices against the toughest competitors or those companies regarded as leaders.

DAVID T. KEARNS, CEO, XEROX CORPORATION

*B*enchmarking is a method of comparing processes, products, and services against organizations with the best practices. You can benchmark best practices to identify how others achieve outstanding results, and can even benchmark the actual measurable outcomes. Doing both is the ideal. This is how it is done.

PLANNING

1. What do you want to benchmark? Take your cues from problem areas, which might include:
- sales;
- market share;
- costs;
- returns;
- customer complaints.

2. What information do you need? Determine which issues are most important, considering, perhaps:

- quality;
- speed;
- cost-effectiveness;
- safety;
- morale.

3. Who will collect the data? For the survey to be both objective and accurate, you will need two or more people. Include colleagues who

- have done benchmarking and surveys before;
- will be authorizing the resulting changes in operation;
- will be implementing the changes.

4. How will you collect the data? Methods include:

- printed survey forms;
- interviews in person or by telephone;
- observation of workplace behaviour.

5. How will you record the data? The benchmarking team will need to develop one or all of:

- appropriate questions;
- survey forms;
- data collection checklists or record sheets.

6. Where will you get the data? Possible sources include:

- professional or industry associations;
- published articles and books;
- conferences and trade shows;
- people in your own organization;
- staff from competing firms;
- people who previously worked for competitors.

ORGANIZING

7. Hold a planning meeting with your team members, using their input to refine the preliminary plan. Get as many people involved as possible, to "spread" the ownership.

8. Find information sources. In some cases, you might solicit co-operation by offering to share your final data.

IMPLEMENTATION

9. Carry out collection of the data according to your plan.

10. Analyze the information you have collected.

11. Organize the data to identify
- where your organization needs to improve;
- how much improvement is required.

12. Determine why your organization is not meeting the benchmark (is it lacking, for example, in staff performance, operation methods, equipment, or materials?).

13. Your organization's efficiency will be most realistically evaluated when you have done your research thoroughly and consistently.

PLANNING FOR CHANGE

14. Set achievement goals for your improvement plan.

15. Develop the plan, including pinpointing what needs to be done, who will do it, and when they will do it.

SELLING THE PLAN

16. Make the "sales" presentation to those who will be authorizing and implementing the plan.

17. Present the team's findings, including goals, solutions, and benefits, to the audience.

18. Obtain authorization for changes in procedures and for any required expenditure.

IMPLEMENTING THE SOLUTION AND BENEFITS

19. Put the improvement plan into action.

20. Monitor implementation procedures to ensure that they are meeting goals.

EVALUATION

21. Measure the results and determine whether goals have been achieved.

22. Give recognition to all the people who helped plan and carry out the project.

Continue to compare performance with current industry benchmarks. Make your organization a leader!

Career

Considering Making a Change?

When the windows of opportunity appear,
don't pull down the shade.

UNKNOWN

*O*rganizations are learning to respond to the demands of the global market by outsourcing, downsizing, and making acquisitions. This has had dramatic consequences for career-minded people. Loyalties are important but tend to be short-term. People need to be flexible and able to adapt themselves to constantly changing job situations.

1. Here are some issues to think about as you contemplate your future in your organization:

- *What are my values?* Your values are the things you appreciate in your relationship with your employer and fellow employees. Some are more important to you than others. These values include such things as honesty, integrity, fairness, and collegiality. When these core values are violated, you may lose your enthusiasm for the company and begin to perform poorly. Write your values down. Then compare them with those that are practised, not preached. When you consider moving to a new job, you need to find out how that organization measures up to your expectations.

- *What special skills and talents do I have?* Keep an inventory of your talents and skills. Make a list of all the courses you have been to and how you may have applied the skills you were taught. Have you special skills that are not commonplace in the market? Think about the type of organization that might bend over backwards to have someone like you work for them.
- *How tolerant am I of risk?* Changing jobs is always a risk. Think about the consequences of the job not working out. How would you feel about being unemployed for a few months? What kind of support do you have at home? What is the extent of your savings to tide you through a rough period? What are your most important needs? What are you looking for in a job? Is it the freedom to make decisions? A need for camaraderie? Security? Low stress? With some effort on your part, could you have your needs met more than they are at present? Or is another organization more capable of doing so?
- *What kind of job will release my highest energy endorphins?* What gets you most excited? What type of job gets you excited each day when you get up? What situation will make you want to work long hours without feeling excessive fatigue?
- *What is my frustration tolerance?* There will always be a period of adjustment in a new job. How well do you adjust to new situations? Can you "roll with the punches"? If so, you should be able to handle more frequent changes in your career.

2. List what you enjoy about your career. Note what aspects of your job you enjoy. Do you like
   - your fellow workers?
   - the challenge?
   - the autonomy?

3. If it is a struggle to find something you really like, you may need a change. List what you would like from your ideal career, no matter what field it might be in.
- What rewards would it provide?
- What sorts of jobs would you be doing?
- How big an organization would you work for?
- What kind of people would you work with?
- What would the work environment be like?

4. Compare the two lists. How many aspects of your ideal career are missing from your present job? How important are those aspects?

5. List the most important needs that are not being met by your current job. Post this list in a prominent place, where you can refer to it often.

6. Seek out information on other organizations, or other departments within your own company, that might give you more job satisfaction than you have now.

7. Create a new list, one based on your career ideals and research, which states
- your first choice of an organization and/or industry;
- your second choice;
- obstacles that must be overcome before moving to the new company or field;
- steps towards overcoming these obstacles, with target dates.

8. Picture yourself in your ideal job, then evaluate it carefully. List good points and bad, assigning a weight to each item. Add up your scores and decide if it's worth moving, or if you should stay in your present position.

9. Fear of change is really fear of the unknown. Consider the worst that might happen. Is it worse than your present position? Then consider what the best possible outcome might be. Chances are the answer will charge you with the energy you need to proceed.

10. If you get a job offer and are uncertain whether to accept it, get advice from people who
- have won your trust;
- demonstrate good judgement;
- have themselves made a career change;
- are impartial about the outcome.

11. Make another list, focusing this time on what your ideal organization would offer in terms of
- salary;
- benefits;
- hours of work;
- location;
- availability of transportation.

12. Discuss your thoughts about career change with your life partner. Make sure that you will get moral support, and that both of you can tolerate the possibility of your being jobless for a period.

13. Find a mentor with whom to discuss your ideas. Have him or her act as a sounding board.

14. Get career counselling. A professional may put you through some tests that will determine your suitability for another career, or may recommend that you stay within your current specialty, even though you may want to change employers.

15. Invest in some self-help books. These often have exercises that will help you arrive at conclusions about your career of which you may not have been aware.

CHANGE DURING
A TAKEOVER

Be prepared for changes thrust on you in the event of a re-organization, a re-engineering exercise, or a takeover. Here's what to expect in a takeover:

— Rumours abound.
— Executives are inaccessible and are in meetings continuously.
— Information from management, in the form of a memo, will usually reflect what people know already.
— No direct reliable information is available from high-profile managers.
— Senior managers resign.
— New faces begin to appear during walking tours.
— A new management team is announced.
— The managers make some attempt to listen to staff.
— New procedures and processes are decreed.
— Further layoffs and resignations take place.
— The culture of the organization changes significantly.

Career
Getting Ahead in Your Organization

My grandfather once told me that there are two kinds of people: those who do the work and those who take the credit. He told me to try to be in the first group; there was less competition there.

INDIRA GANDHI

No one can manage your career better than you can. But if you wait for opportunities to present themselves, you may sit around forever. You must be pro-active. You must be assertive. The following ideas will improve your chances of moving up the corporate ladder.

1. Make yourself indispensable. Create a niche by doing things that others can't or may not want to do.

2. Go the extra mile. Help out in a crisis. Put extra effort in if a project is late. Be seen to be helpful. Help during emergencies.

3. Make your boss look good. You will be valued and appreciated. And if you do enough good, the favours will be returned, sooner or later.

4. Know what your boss's goals are, then modify your behaviour to do things that will advance your boss's goals.

5. Work more effectively when you're not supervised. The next time your boss is out of the office, such as when she is on holiday, exceed her expectations by having projects completed. Leave a note on her desk or on her voice mail, so that she has the assurance and peace of mind that things are in good hands.

6. Exceed the specifications of your job as laid out in your job description. Regularly document the things you are doing that are not described. At your next performance review, make your boss aware of your extra work, so your job description will be updated. Your boss will then be forced to acknowledge your growth.

7. Do something special and have it published. Document your success and write an article about it. After passing it by your boss, find a publisher or a magazine you support. A published article will add to your credentials as an expert.

8. In a team situation, be a player and give your best efforts to meeting goals on time and within budget. Encourage other team members to do the same.

9. Be a willing volunteer, especially for projects that will let you prove your abilities to senior staff and key decision-makers.

10. Avoid politics. You cannot expect to exert more than minimal influence on the people you oppose. If you are pushed to take sides, hold off until you can pick the likely winner.

11. Understand the big picture. This will give you a sense of where opportunities are developing.

12. Find out how people who have been promoted did it.

13. Become the most technically competent employee in your area. Have your peers cross-train you. If necessary, do it on your own time.

14. Focus on excelling in your existing job. Don't obsess about looking for opportunities outside the organization. If you must, read the Career Planning section, quit, and find another job!

15. Project a positive attitude at all times.

16. Volunteer for task forces, particularly those that have a high profile in the organization.

17. Train, train, and train some more. Get as much education as you can to enhance your ability on the job. Take courses that might be useful to your peers, then offer to present a summary of what you have learned to them. Offer to cross-train others.

18. Teach, teach, teach — become a mentor to someone else and help that person grow.

19. Be assertive in getting your career goals known. Ask for promotions and opportunities whenever it feels appropriate.

20. Develop a picture of what you want to be doing five years down the road. Make a list of roadblocks that might prevent you from being successful. Develop action plans to overcome these obstacles over a period of time. Communicate these to your boss.

21. Be honest. Your reputation for integrity will compensate for the occasional awkwardness of telling the truth.

22. Collaborate with those around you. Co-operative people are more likely to get promotions than those who are constantly in conflict with their co-workers.

23. Focus on the big picture. Be aware of important current issues and industry trends, and find new ways to help your organization succeed. Identify obstacles to corporate performance, and make suggestions on how to overcome them.

24. Seek out a mentor, a respected person in your organization whom you see as a role model. Choose someone whose skills and person-ality will give you an opportunity to learn different approaches and techniques. Consult your mentor for advice and feedback, especially when you have difficult decisions to make.

25. Discuss your career goals with your boss so that you agree on both their suitability and the route by which you plan to achieve them. Ask for feedback on whether your plans are realistic, and for advice on what training you might need to gain the necessary skills.

26. Set goals and develop your career action plan around them, using mini-goals to track your progress. Review goals regularly, and make adjustments to your plan if you get off-track.

27. Be positive. If you have doubts about a project, don't present them as impassable obstacles. Maintain the position that there are no problems, only opportunities and solutions. Optimists achieve more because of their "can do" attitude, while negative people rarely succeed.

28. Dress for success. Dress for the role you want, not for the one you have.

29. Follow up on your promises. Underpromise and overdeliver.

30. Put your energies into projects that
- use your skills;
- are likely to succeed;
- require major effort and resources.

31. Work visibly to help your organization succeed.

32. Be generous with useful tips and sales leads.

33. Research and report on ways to reduce costs.

34. Be the person who knows what's happening. Become a source of information on current trends by reading trade and business-news publications and passing on useful material to your colleagues.

35. Take on projects that others don't want to do. Your boss and your associates will appreciate you.

36. If a situation is occurring that might embarrass or anger your boss, be the one to break the news as soon as possible. Your boss will appreciate being prepared for unpleasant outcomes.

37. Maintain up-to-date information about your boss's expectations of you. Make sure that performance goals can be measured, so your achievements will be clearly perceived.

38. Request increasing levels of authority and autonomy, and then prove yourself worthy of them. It may be a stretch, but you will be able to prove how capable you are to yourself and others.

39. Do better by competing against yourself, rather than your peers. Competitiveness breeds resentment. Strive for your personal best, and let others judge you against your peers.

40. Ask key people for feedback. Listen to them without being defensive. Show your appreciation by demonstrating improved performance.

41. Take a positive approach when criticized.
- Be as objective and unemotional as possible. Avoid defensiveness.
- Consider the critic's point of view.
- Use criticism as a learning opportunity.
- Reflect on the criticism. If you think it unfair, defend yourself.
- Thank the critic, even if you disagree with the evaluation.

42. If you are fired or demoted, learn from the experience. Rather than trying to establish blame, find out what went wrong. Try as hard as you can to be objective, fix the problem if you can, and make sure you don't make the same mistake again.

43. Win support by thanking in public those who help you.

44. Learn to get what you want without alienating the people you meet. You never know who might affect your future career path.

45. Take advantage of a possible upcoming job vacancy and put yourself in the lead by
- taking on extra work that will demonstrate relevant skills;
- letting key people know you are interested;
- making sure your skills are updated to match the vacancy.

46. Take the initiative. Go beyond the "normal" course of duty and do things that make a difference.

47. Gain a larger perspective. Look at your organization from the viewpoint of the customer, the owners, and the staff. Try to balance often-conflicting needs.

48. Take responsibility. Show leadership. Identify yourself as one who will demonstrate the values of your organization. Project a "can do" attitude.

49. Be a team player. Work collaboratively. Help others to excel. They will return the favour when you least expect it or when you might need it.

50. Present your ideas with panache. Tell your story with enthusiasm, always taking into account the needs of your audience.

Career

Your attitude always determines your altitude in life.

SUCCESSORIES INC.

To climb in your career you must be clear about your personal goals, learn how to add value, and develop skills you can take anywhere. As more people enter the information age, change is happening at an ever-increasing pace. As knowledge workers begin to predominate, new skills sets will become important. You must hone your skills in these areas:

INTUITION

1. Develop your ability to have insight that goes beyond facts and figures. Numbers rule and logic may tell you one thing, but your observations, questions, and perception may reveal new opportunities. Step back and look at the big picture. Try to ignore the details.

EMPATHY

2. Learn to understand issues from the viewpoint of those around you. Begin to "feel" issues from the perspective of people who are from a different cultural, religious, or gender background from you. And make allowances for those differences.

VISIONING

3. Develop an understanding about where you and those who work with you could and should be a few years ahead. Think about it . . . What differentiated Martin Luther King, John F. Kennedy, Nelson Mandela, and Mahatma Gandhi from us mere mortals? They had vision. Equally important, they were able to communicate their vision to those around them in a compelling manner and excite and mobilize people. Having a vision is of limited value unless we share it and excite other people.

FLEXIBILITY

4. Have an open mind when change must be made. More important, anticipate the future. Preparing for the future and making adjustments in our attitudes and procedures will ensure that change is constant, not periodic and traumatic.

PRO-ACTIVITY

5. Get things done. Find the easy way. Don't get analysis paralysis. Sure, you often need information before making a decision, but doing things and modifying and learning as you go along can often pay much higher dividends. There is another benefit — people will realize that making a mistake is not bad, it's an opportunity to learn and improve. Doing nothing will cause disillusionment and could become part of the culture.

SEEING THE BIG PICTURE

6. Step away from the daily grind to see your organization in the context of the economy, its industry, its direction, its leadership, and its competitors.

PARTNERING

7. Learn to work collaboratively. Partner with people from other work areas. Share the rewards and recognition. Develop partnerships with people outside your organization, especially those who can add value to your endeavours.

LIFE-LONG LEARNING

8. Take every opportunity to learn new skills and get new ideas. Courses, inside and outside the organization, are only a small part of accumulating knowledge. Reading books, attending conferences, subscribing to trade magazines, and learning from your mistakes will help too.

Career

You never get a second chance to make a first impression.

UNKNOWN

Getting an interview for a job is usually the last of a number of difficult steps that might produce a job offer. This is showtime — an opportunity for you to sell yourself. You will probably come up against a professional who knows the difference between glib catchphrases and substance, so be prepared to leave the interviewer with no doubt that you are the best person for the job. Here's how to give yourself the best appearance:

IN PREPARATION FOR THE INTERVIEW

1. Find out everything you can about the company. This will demonstrate a genuine interest in the organization and an affinity for the things that its employees do. Your research should include information on the nature of the business; how well the company is doing; changes in the industry, with particular focus on things that could influence your job; the size of the company; and the diversity of products and services provided.

2. Create a list of questions you want to ask. You should avoid asking about salaries at an early stage. Your questions should instead reflect an interest in the company and an awareness of your contribution to its future. Questions could include:

- How is the organization doing?
- What is the outlook for business over the next five years?
- How would you describe the culture here?
- How do people get recognized for superior performance, outside the formal compensation system?
- How important is teamwork in your organization?
- What kind of training does the organization provide?
- How readily does the organization embrace new technology and other improved working systems?
- How are employees kept informed of changes in the organization?
- What would be the primary reason for people leaving the organization in the last year or two?
- Are there some characteristics common to people who have been promoted in the organization?

3. Review your resumé to ensure that it contains as many things that could be of interest to the company as possible.

4. If you do have more than one interview, schedule them with sufficient time in between to avoid rushing from one to the other.

5. Collect and organize all supporting documentation, such as certificates of your professional qualifications and references.

6. Be sure you have accurate directions to the prospective employer, to ensure that you don't spend time searching for the place and arriving stressed.

7. Consider doing a role-play with a friend. Have him ask you some challenging, open-ended questions that require on-the-spot mental acrobatics. Questions could include:

- "In your last job, what would be the one thing that your peers most disliked about you?"
- "What would be your single most important achievement in your last job?"
- "How would you describe yourself?"
- "What type of training could the company provide you with, to make you a better contributor?"
- "What attracted you to this job?"
- "What do you know about the company?"
- "What would you like to tell me in support of your application, other than what is on your resumé?"
- "Can you give me examples of initiatives that you have taken in your previous job that were above and beyond what your job description required you to do?"

ON THE DAY OF YOUR INTERVIEW

8. Dress for success.

- Make sure that you are well groomed. Your hair should be neat and you should be cleanly shaven.
- Your clothes should reflect the fact that you are a neat person. They should be clean and well pressed. Be sure to fix any loose buttons and hems.
- Avoid outlandish hairstyles and body ornamentation that may not be in keeping with the culture of the organization you want to work for.
- Avoid clothing that is too revealing, frilly, or makes you look much taller than you actually are.

9. Leave yourself extra time to get to the interview.

10. Have all supporting documentation ready, including your resumé, references, and non-confidential documentation of work you have done that would demonstrate your ability to do the job.

11. Bring writing materials so you can make notes on important issues. Don't rely on your memory, particularly if you have any other interviews on that day.

12. Introduce yourself. Give your interviewer a firm handshake. Smile. Look relaxed. Make small talk to establish rapport that seems genuine, such as "I love this location! It's so easy to get to." Or "It must be my lucky day. The traffic was so much lighter than usual coming in."

13. Let the interviewer control the discussion. Listen carefully to her questions. Show that you understand by nodding and paraphrasing difficult questions.

14. Do not ramble when responding to open-ended questions. Try to be as direct as possible. If you are not sure that you have answered the question, ask if the interviewer has the answer that he was looking for, and if not, what he would like you to deal with.

15. Look and act interested. Sit slightly forward and maintain eye contact, without staring.

16. Pay attention to what the interviewer says. Equally important, watch non-verbal cues. Look for facial expressions that might indicate confusion with your answers, such as loss of eye contact or change in voice pitch. Crossing arms or legs may mean resistance. Leaning forward or nodding might mean enthusiasm. (*See* Communicating: Reading Body Language.)

17. Project a great attitude. Show your "can do" enthusiasm by
- always accentuating the positive;
- giving examples of the good things you have done.

18. Project positive body language. This will mean that you
- smile warmly when greeted;
- maintain eye contact, without staring;
- greet people with a firm handshake;
- stand tall or sit up straight, so you project enthusiasm and confidence;
- avoid putting your hand in front of your face while you are talking or fidgeting when you are listening;
- never smoke or chew gum.

19. Speak to impress by
- articulating key ideas with a firmer voice;
- avoiding rushing through answers and rambling;
- avoiding slang or swear words;
- avoiding annoying words such as "like" at the beginning, middle, and end of each sentence.

20. Listen. Make sure you answer all questions adequately. When you are not sure if you have done this, ask, "Have I answered your question?" This will indicate that you care about responding fully.

21. If you don't understand a question, ask for clarification.

22. Stay calm and confident. You got the interview, now get the job!

23. Use examples wherever possible. This will demonstrate a "can do" approach. It will also increase the interviewer's confidence that you can do the job in practice, rather than in theory.

24. Close the meeting decisively. Consider using a sentence such as "I've enjoyed the discussion. Where do we go from here?"

BE PREPARED TO ANSWER THESE QUESTIONS

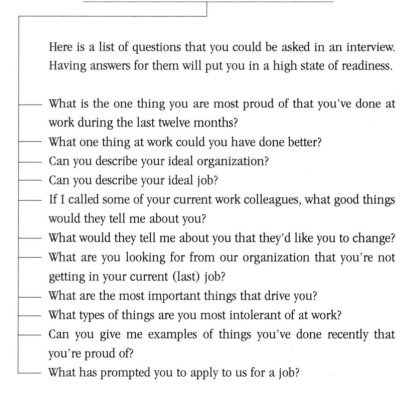

Here is a list of questions that you could be asked in an interview. Having answers for them will put you in a high state of readiness.

- What is the one thing you are most proud of that you've done at work during the last twelve months?
- What one thing at work could you have done better?
- Can you describe your ideal organization?
- Can you describe your ideal job?
- If I called some of your current work colleagues, what good things would they tell me about you?
- What would they tell me about you that they'd like you to change?
- What are you looking for from our organization that you're not getting in your current (last) job?
- What are the most important things that drive you?
- What types of things are you most intolerant of at work?
- Can you give me examples of things you've done recently that you're proud of?
- What has prompted you to apply to us for a job?

Career Planning

Know thyself.

SOCRATES

Career planning is about improving your current job or seeking the next one. It is about a work and life balance — life management. It is about relationships with your boss and your colleagues. Here is how you can enhance your career.

1. Stay informed about new and current trends.
   • Become a member of professional associations.
   • Read books and journals in your area of expertise.

2. Attend seminars, workshops, conferences, and trade shows.

3. Promote new ideas, so you won't be seen as someone who is afraid of change.

4. Be open to change and eager to try new ideas. Ask to sit on committees dealing with new technologies.

5. Update your resumé frequently, highlighting your successes and major achievements. Be sure to include projects that added measurable value to your department or organization. Don't be afraid to blow your own horn.

6. Take every training course you can manage — they all have something new to offer. Include them on your resumé, and make sure your boss is aware of your professional-development activities and their worth to the company.

7. Add to your network of business associates. Stay in touch and make them aware of your present activities and future career plans.

8. Make contact with people who know where the employment opportunities are, both inside and outside your organization. Add professional recruiters to your network.

9. Determine your monetary value in the marketplace. If you find you are not being paid enough, you will be motivated to try for a raise or for a position with another firm. Three factors decide your worth:
   • the need for your work;
   • your ability to do the job;
   • the difficulty of replacing you.

10. Evaluate your strengths. What are you especially good at? Find out if key people agree with your analysis.

11. Focus on skills you have, or might acquire, that are unique in the organization. Fluency in foreign languages or knowledge of particular computer applications are possible examples.

Change

It does not matter how small you are
if you have faith and a plan of action.

FIDEL CASTRO

We all know how hard change is, but adapting to change can be challenging and fun. Here's how you can make the transition easier, and benefit from opportunities that may be presented.

1. Look to the future. Anticipate change and its potential impact on your work area.

2. Be optimistic about change. Look at it as an opportunity and a challenge rather than a threat. Think about how you could benefit rather than what you stand to lose. Focus on the opportunities that might come your way. For example, people tend to move to jobs with more stability during turbulent times. This will give you an opportunity to expand your job or, better still, apply for a better job that has been vacated.

3. Keep your ear close to the ground, so you are aware of pending change. Find out how significant it will be. Determine the following:

- Who will be affected?
- How significant is the change?
- Is the change organizational, legal, technological, or procedural?
- Is the change urgent?

4. Try to understand change in the context of the "big picture." Review the company's mission and vision on your own or with your boss. This will give you a context within which the changes make sense.

5. Ask your boss if you can go to a workshop on change. You will learn some new coping skills to make the transition easier.

6. Show people how they can benefit from change. If the task requires more effort, skill, or responsibility, provide rewards such as higher pay, more time off, or specialized training.

7. Listen to your colleagues' ideas on how to make change as smooth as possible. Their advice could prove invaluable.

8. Some of your plans for change will fail. Treat failure as a learning experience. Analyze what you did wrong, so you don't make the same mistake again.

9. Be conscientious of your own reaction to change. Typically, people go through four phases:
- denial;
- anger;
- acceptance;
- action.

Work quickly through the first three phases to get yourself into an action mode.

Change

Becoming a Champion

*You may be disappointed if you fail;
trust you are doomed if you don't try.*

BEVERLY SILLS

*In life, always tell yourself that things are fine as they are, but
would be even better if they were different.*

JEAN-PAUL FILION

Change is a fact of life in the new millennium. Those who are waiting for the dust to settle are living in a world of fantasy. Change will continue, with one difference — it will happen more often and it will take place in bigger increments. You must adapt or die like the dinosaur. Here are some strategies to help you become the master, not the slave.

AVOID BEING JUDGEMENTAL

1. Keep an open mind about situations and events around you. Don't allow personal prejudices to cloud your vision. Don't rush to judgement. Listen and let yourself be influenced rather than clouding

your mind with rebuttals. Give others the benefit of the doubt. Ask yourself if your resistance is based on fact or on a personal bias.

KEEP ON LEARNING

2. You're never too old to learn. In fact, we can learn something every day. Don't wait for the classroom — learn from your mistakes. Maintain an attitude of inquisitiveness. Find out everything there is to know from those willing to share. Read voraciously — books, magazines, the Internet. Jot down key points of interest and keep them in a file to review regularly.

LOOK FOR THE NEXT TREND

3. Trends and fads are not the same, nor are they necessarily bad. The fact is that organizations, like people, follow trends. By observing and learning about what is new, you can position yourself as an expert and take a leadership role in making changes. This will give you greater control of the changes.

FOSTER A RESOURCE NETWORK

4. Continually expand your sources of help and information. Keep in touch with people whose careers are taking off. Find out what they are doing, that perhaps you are not. Subscribe to magazines that stay on the leading edge. Look for key articles each month.

BE A PROBLEM-SOLVER, NOT A PROBLEM-CREATOR

5. Anyone can spend his life identifying problems. There are more than enough to go around. Pointing these out can become tiresome to the people around you, particularly if they respond with "It's not my job." Be willing to identify solutions if there is a problem, and consider making time to solve it. This will earn you a reputation as a "fixer" — the kind of person chosen for promotions.

ENJOY YOURSELF

6. Have fun. Laugh a lot. It's contagious. Life's too short not to have fun. People work better when they are enjoying themselves. And humour enables everyone to relax and open themselves to change.

KEEP A POSITIVE ATTITUDE

7. Every new situation can be looked at in one of two ways: as a problem or as an opportunity. Choose the highway, not the byway. Make each challenge an opportunity to test your intellect and resilience.

SHOW INDEPENDENCE

8. Some people are dependent and others independent. Dependent people point to others when they are challenged. They say, "You screwed up," "It's not my responsibility," "You decide." Independent people say, "I'll fix it," "I'll take responsibility," or "I'll make the time." Be willing to step up to the plate. No one ever learned to play the game from the bleachers.

Change
Surviving a Corporate Merger

Just when I was getting used to yesterday,
along came today.

ANONYMOUS

*M*ergers and alliances between organizations are being spurred on by a booming stock market and increased globalization. As they are becoming a common feature of the corporate landscape, it is necessary for people to have a strategy to deal pro-actively with the consequences. Here are some things you can do:

BEFORE A MERGER

1.
- Prepare for the worst at all times. This is not about being a pessimist, but about being a realist. Update your resumé regularly, adding special achievements.
- Maintain an extensive network of people who could assist you to relocate.
- Upgrade your skills at regular intervals. Take advantage of any opportunity to learn the latest and greatest in your field of expertise.

2.

- Accept that you will have to deal with uncertainty. This is far better than wishing that the situation wasn't so or looking for scapegoats for your unhappiness.
- Keep yourself busy. This will give you less time to believe every new rumour.
- Prepare yourself for the new culture. Find out all you can about the organization you are merging with, particularly if it is the larger of the two. Get a sense of the corporate culture of the other company through networking and reading published annual reports at your stockbroker's, the library, or on the Internet. Specifically, find out whether it has acquired or merged with other organizations before, what has transpired with regards to rationalizing operations, and how people have been treated. This will give you a clue as to what to expect.
- Try to understand why the two organizations are getting together. This will give you some ability to forecast likely changes. A merger between companies with overlapping markets could suggest more layoffs than one between organizations that complement one another.
- Treat the changes as an opportunity. A lot of good people might bolt, leaving increased chances for additional responsibilities and promotions.
- Invariably, many of the details of how to capitalize on the merger will be finalized in the trenches. Task forces will be set up to examine new opportunities or merge interests. Being on a task force will give you additional ability to control the future and will keep you informed about likely changes before they happen. It will also give you the opportunity to demonstrate your enthusiasm to people in a position of influence.

- Assess your value in the marketplace. If you have a skill that is in high demand, sit tight. Resigning will be less profitable than sticking around for a financial package.
- On the other hand, if you feel vulnerable and have skills that are neither in demand nor likely to fit into the new situation, you would be advised to begin a job search as insurance.
- Finally, if you have a good relationship with your boss, talk to her in confidence and share your concerns. Ask for her help and guidance.

Coaching
Your Teammates

*The final test of a leader is that he leaves behind
in other men the conviction and the will to carry on.*

*W*hile your immediate boss is expected to be your coach, the span of control of managers is becoming so great that they are having difficulty helping their people. This creates opportunities for people to help each other improve their jobs in an informal way. Here's how you can contribute to your work area's success by assisting your co-workers.

1. Share your technical knowledge with those around you. This will improve productivity. It will also demonstrate your collaborative skills — something that could help you secure a promotion.

2. If your boss is very busy, offer to take new associates under your wing. Show them the ropes. Introduce them to their peers and key people in other departments. Help them to start off well by showing them the best of what the organization has to offer. This will assure them that they have not made a mistake by joining your organization.

3. Get detailed instructions from your boss. Find out specifically
   - who needs to be trained;
   - what they need to know;
   - when you should begin and complete the training;
   - where the training should take place;
   - why training is needed;
   - how they should be trained.

4. Meet with the trainee. Find out
   - his confidence level;
   - any previous training that he has had;
   - what concerns he might have;
   - any special needs.

5. Increase your associates' skills by
   - explaining what you want them to do;
   - showing them how to do it;
   - letting them try while you observe;
   - giving them feedback on their performance;
   - making them aware if their performance has not met the standards expected.

6. If associates fail to do the job right, redirect them. Show them again. Ask them to confirm their understanding. Have them demonstrate their understanding by showing you how to do the task.

7. If the task is large or appears difficult, break it into smaller pieces. Learning one stage at a time will build the trainee's self-confidence.

8. If your new associate struggles with English, help her by writing down instructions in language that is

- simple;
- point by point;
- free of jargon;
- enhanced with pictures and diagrams wherever possible.

9. The more complex the task, the more important it is that you document your instructions. When you do, make sure that the instructions
- are easy to follow;
- use simple language;
- follow a logical sequence;
- complement diagrams wherever needed;
- are in point form.

10. Give people regular feedback. Wherever possible, measure their performance so that they know when they are improving or getting worse.

Commitment

Team

Never doubt that a small group of thoughtful,
committed people can change the world.
Indeed, it is the only thing that ever has.

SUCCESSORIES INC.

*W*inning commitment to a project is a real challenge, especially when you are dealing with a team of your peers. Here are some approaches to get them to buy into the process:

1. Make sure you know exactly what commitment is required before you try to sell the project to your team. If you are confused about it, you will lose credibility with the group.

2. Set up a team meeting and explain the project to the team members. Be sure to give a clear picture of the desired outcome.

3. Sell the benefits of completing the project on time and within the budget.

4. Listen respectfully to your colleagues' legitimate concerns. Show that you understand their feelings.

5. Evaluate the strength of the team's buy-in. Record members' concerns on a flip chart to ensure that everyone understands the issues.

6. Work with your team to remove obstacles to success. Ask for ideas for solving problems that the team can handle, and offer your own ideas for areas where you have control.

7. Get the team as a whole to work out criteria for measuring progress and determining when the project goal has been reached.

8. Determine the long- and shorter-term goals of the project, and get them approved by the appropriate level(s) of management.

9. Get team members to describe how their efforts will contribute to reaching goals, and find out what they expect of their colleagues.

10. Have each team member confirm his or her commitment to the project. When procedures and steps have been agreed upon, write up action plans (who, what, and by when) in the minutes and circulate copies to all members.

Communicating

In Writing

Writing without thinking is like
shooting without aiming.

ARNOLD GLASGOW

*M*ost job descriptions include a requirement for effective communication skills, both oral and written. Sadly, many people find it difficult to express their ideas on paper, and thus to communicate effectively both inside and outside their organizations. Here are some suggestions for improving your writing skills:

1. Think before you write. Could what you need to communicate be better expressed verbally? The most important reasons for written documentation are: an important decision must be made; you are dealing with a complex issue; the material must be studied before a decision is made.

2. Write your material in a logical sequence:
   - At the beginning, state the reason why it was written.
   - Next, especially in the case of an action memo, let all people who read the document know what is expected of them.
   - Finally, provide the information required by the readers.

3. Be brief and to the point — your key ideas should stand out clearly.

4. Begin by letting readers know the value of your note. Entice them with introductions such as "This report will reveal how the corporation can save up to $15 million!"

5. Try to give a positive spin to your message. For example, you can make a statement such as "Company policy requires that you do not smoke in the building" a more positive statement by saying, "You are welcome to smoke in the courtyard."

6. Show readers how the benefits will impact on them. Converting an "I" into a "you" can often do this. For example, "I know we can offer significant advantages over our competition" can be changed to "We would be pleased to demonstrate the benefits you will receive."

7. Let your readers know at all times that you have a keen sense of what *their* needs are. This will motivate them to take the actions you require.

8. Keep paragraphs short, especially the first one. If the material looks easy to read, the recipients will get into the meat of the document before they know it. Vary the length of paragraphs throughout the piece, but try to keep all of them relatively short.

9. Avoid clogging your document with details. Save background and technical material for attachments or appendices. Alert your readers to their existence by referring to them: "See Attachment A."

10. Use plain language and avoid jargon, unless it is part of your readers' normal vocabulary.

11. Avoid repetition. Draw attention to important ideas by formatting and placement within the document.

12. Send copies to relevant colleagues only. People who receive copies without expecting them will be confused and may suspect you of playing office politics.

13. Model your writing on excellent examples. Make copies of writing that impresses you and keep them on file.

14. Avoid gender bias in your writing. The following techniques are useful when dealing with the difficult "he/she" problem:
- Use plural subjects. For example, "The manager should meet regularly with his salesmen" could be expressed as "Managers should meet regularly with their salespeople."
- Use plural or neutral pronouns. For example, "No man is an island" could become "No one is an island," or even "We are not islands."
- Use neutral nouns instead of singular pronouns. For example, "Ask him who knows" could become "Ask the person who knows."
- Avoid possessive pronouns. For example, "The manager should tell his people" could be expressed as "The manager should tell staff."

15. Write as if you are speaking with your colleagues. A conversational style is more approachable and readable than stilted, formal language.

16. Read your work aloud to see if it sounds right. Make changes if necessary, and read it aloud again until it works.

Communicating
Using E-mail

I apologize for the length of this letter.
If there had been sufficient time, I'd have made it shorter.

GOETHE

E-mail is fast replacing faxes and regular mail as the primary written form of communication. The ability to send messages around the world in seconds possesses real advantages over other forms of communication, so one can expect this form of communication to grow at a very rapid rate. Using e-mail effectively will improve the way others view you. Use these tips to be an effective modern-day communicator.

1. Make communicating responses a priority — particularly those required by clients. It will impress them. Responding on the same day is ideal — within the hour will impress the hell out of them!

2. Keep your communications less formal than you normally would. For example, it is not necessary to let people know that you are replying to their letter of such and such a date. They already know these details.

3. Keep your messages short. This will not only reduce your composition and downloading time, but will also save the reader uploading time and needless eyestrain.

4. If your message is long, consider sending it as an attachment, enabling the reader to review it off-line.

5. Write in short paragraphs to get clear messages across. Leave a blank line between paragraphs to make it clear when you are changing thoughts or topics.

6. Always include a title in the subject line. Make your title concise and compelling.

7. Use the "cc" box if you feel that your information may be of interest to others. However, if you'd rather not let the reader know that you're sending the e-mail to others, include these people in your "bcc" box.

8. Avoid sending sound and pictures unless you are able to compress them. Failure to do so will extend the downloading time considerably and cause your reader annoyance.

9. Print and keep a hard copy of important e-mails and your responses to them.

10. Don't use all capital letters. It isn't done regularly and shouldn't be done in e-mail. People feel as if you are shouting at them.

11. While e-mails appear private, they are not. They may be passed on

to or retrieved by people with whom you had no intention of
communicating. Be careful of your language and humour.

12. Be mindful of the messages you pass on. Do so very selectively.
Messages about virus warnings and contests may interest or amuse
you, but they can be annoying to others. Seek people's permission to
download information that is outside the boundaries of your regular
communications.

13. When replying, double-check to ensure that you are sending your
response only to Person A, and not to a group listserv.

14. Don't include a full text of what you received in your return mail
unless it's short. Instead, consider copying only those parts that you
are replying to.

15. The better e-mail programs allow you to filter unwanted e-mails.
Others that may be less important can be dumped into a folder for
review when you have some spare time.

Communicating

Within an Active Grapevine

*The nice part of living in a small town
is that when I don't know what I'm doing,
someone else does.*

ANONYMOUS

We live in times of turbulent change. People need information to make sense of the things they don't understand. As management typically reacts to these needs, the grapevine will fill in the information gaps for people. Some of the information you will get is true, but a lot will not be. Here are some ways of dealing with the informal information that swirls around you.

AVOID RUMOURS

1.
- Take the attitude that it is better to give too much information than too little.
- Hold regular briefings. By definition, they should be short. They can be, for example, stand-up meetings in the office or a huddle on the factory floor. If you don't have new information, encourage questions, which may uncover rumours you are not aware of.

- Keep a flip chart in your work area. Write news on it regularly. Allow your people to record questions that they want to deal with at your meetings.
- Anticipate issues that might provoke negative gossip. Deal with them right away.

DEAL WITH RUMOURS

2.
- Never deny the truth or lie. Your credibility will suffer, and trust between you and other people will be jeopardized. Often information reaches others before you get it. Try to track down the source and establish whether the information is truth or fiction. When you have the facts, let people know them right away.
- Go to the source of the rumour. Find out if you or your team will be affected. Find ways to position yourself to take advantage of the situation. Develop a plan that will demonstrate how you and your people can help to make the change successful.
- When you go to the source of a rumour, don't demand answers or put people on the spot. Make it easy for them to help you by asking questions that can be dealt with hypothetically. Ask, for example, "If, at some time in the future, there was a downsizing, which departments would be cut first?" Watch their body language when they answer in order to understand how they feel.
- Maintain a positive attitude. Take particular care to do good work, since a deteriorating attitude and work habits will make you stick out like a sore thumb.
- Be flexible to change. Look at all the alternatives. Change brings opportunity. New directions should challenge and energize you.

3. Don't add to the rumour mill. If you are passing on hearsay, do so accurately. If you change the information, qualify if for the recipient by saying that it is your interpretation or opinion.

4. When you are given information that is unofficial and "spicy," check its accuracy by asking:
- Where did you get this information?
- How do you know it is true?
- Is this a fact or is it your opinion?

5. Check the accuracy of important messages with your boss. Be frank. Let him know what you have heard and the extent of your concern.

6. Avoid going to your boss with every bit of hearsay. You will begin to be seen as a rumour-monger. Speak to her about important issues only.

7. If your boss does disclose confidential information to you, maintain that confidentiality at all costs; trust is something you have to work hard at to maintain, but it can be lost quickly.

8. Go to the source to establish the accuracy of a rumour if you feel your boss cannot validate it and
- you feel empowered to do so;
- it impacts you or your team;
- the issue is important.

9. If you find that a rumour is accurate and it will impact your work area, share it with your boss.

10. Help your boss develop a strategy to present your information in a manner that will be least disruptive to your area.

11. Continue to do good work, since any deterioration in your attitude and work habits will make you more vulnerable to any changes that might happen.

12. Be flexible about the outcome of change. Opportunities are bound to present themselves.

13. Most rumours will have little impact on you, but major changes could be coming if you notice that senior managers are

- spending more time in meetings;
- looking worried;
- talking in lower tones among themselves;
- taking phone calls or having more conversations behind closed doors.

Communicating

Reading Body Language

*R*esearch indicates that only 7 percent of a message is communicated with words; 55 percent is transmitted via gestures, and the balance — 38 percent — from tone. Clearly, we need to be more adept at reading non-verbal cues, so our perceptive radar can pick up messages accurately.

1. Body language can be different in different cultures. But in Western societies, there are some clues to the thoughts and feelings of people. Here are some common body postures and what they mean.

- Crossed legs and arms. *Not open to your ideas. Defensive.*
- Darting eyes. *Anxious or lacking confidence.*
- Staring. *Person is not hearing you.*
- Eyes up at top left. *Figuring a way to outmanoeuvre you. May be lying.*
- Eyes up at top right. *Trying to figure something out. Conceptual, silent problem-solving.*
- Hands on hips or hip jutted out. *Confident, almost arrogant. Challenging.*
- Hands at side. *Neutral.*
- Hands closed in a fig-leaf position. *Could indicate a closed attitude.*
- Jacket buttoned up. *Formal.*

- Jacket unbuttoned. *Open, informal.*
- Leaning forward. *Acceptance and interest in what you're saying.*
- Leaning back, arms behind head. *Contemplative, skeptical, possibly with reservations; relaxed.*
- Looking over top of eyeglasses. *Evaluative, skeptical.*
- Open hands, palms down. *Demanding.*
- Open hands, palms up. *Wanting, needing.*
- Hands on the table. *Willingness to get things done.*
- Slouch. *Low self-esteem.*
- Slow blink. *Person doesn't enjoy being there.*
- Smile. *Enjoyment, pleasure.*
- Head angled down. *Shame, shyness, or lying.*
- Head back. *Arrogance or a sense of superiority.*
- Head cocked to the side. *Interested or listening; acceptance of your idea.*

2. In using body language, try always to show a positive, open approach to encourage reciprocity. The best combination might be leaning slightly forward, cocking your head slightly to the side, keeping your arms at your side, and smiling.

Communicating

Informally

Sticks and stones may break our bones,
but words will break our heart.

ROBERT FULGHUM

*B*eing able to make your point is a big step towards influencing others and gaining more control of the world around you. This will increase your motivation, self-esteem, and opportunities for promotion. Here are some ways to improve your communication skills:

1. Pick the proper time and place for a discussion. If these considerations are ignored, you can expect only a limited transfer of information.

2. If you want something, be specific and express yourself clearly.

3. To make sure that people have understood you, ask them to repeat your message back to you in their own words.

4. Choose your words carefully. Avoid words that will trigger a negative reaction.

5. Watch people's faces and body language for their response to your message. Pay special attention to their eyes for signs of confusion, resistance, or lack of understanding. (*See* Communicating: Reading Body Language.)

6. Choose, if possible, a quiet area for your discussion. If there is unavoidable background noise, raise your voice and use gestures to reinforce your words.

7. Vary your manner of speaking in order to keep the other people interested. Retain listeners' attention by changing the volume and speed of your delivery, and by pausing before or after you make an important point.

8. Maintain eye contact with the people you are speaking to, but remember that some cultures find this threatening or rude.

9. Devote all your attention to the conversation at hand. Don't allow phone calls or other people's interruptions to distract you.

10. Listen carefully to what the other people are saying and how they are feeling. Pay close attention to the nuances of their voices, gestures, facial expressions, postures, and eye movements.

11. When you want to make a particularly important point, raise your voice a bit or speak more deliberately. Use body language to reinforce your message by leaning forward, widening your eyes, or using gestures.

12. Always start the conversation on a positive note. The potential for conflict can be reduced by starting with a subject on which you and your listeners agree. This foundation of common interest will

establish an atmosphere of trust that will make it easier to deal with more contentious issues.

13. Try to replace the word "but" with "and." "But" is a word that implies disagreement and dismissal, and using it will make your audience resist your arguments.

14. Use "I" rather than "you." The first-person approach implies that you are willing to be part of the solution. For example, instead of saying "You need to clean up this mess," try "I need some help getting this mess cleared up."

15. Be specific. Avoid phrases such as "We'll get it done soon," and say instead "We'll have it done by Friday at noon."

16. Respect people for their ideas. You don't have to agree with every idea, but you should give others the opportunity to express their opinions. Listen to be influenced. Don't cloud your mind with your own preconceived ideas. Be mindful of the fact that you do have prejudices that may interfere with your ability to appreciate others' opinions.

17. If you have a disagreement with someone, consider
    • emphasizing things you have in common;
    • mirroring the person's body posture, tone of voice, and gestures;
    • agreeing with their feelings even if you disagree with their ideas.

18. Make your message clear. Keep it
    • short;
    • free of jargon and legalese;
    • simple;
    • interesting — add an anecdote that will make it relevant.

19. Confirm understanding and agreement. Ask for periodic feedback. Listen to what others say and judge whether you have whole-hearted agreement or superficial compliance. If it's the latter, you need to ask more questions to find out the reasons for any reluctance.

20. Involve other people in helping to find a solution. Ask them for help even if you had ideas for an appropriate solution. Using their ideas will enhance their buy-in and ownership for a successful outcome.

21. End conversations with a summary so that all parties are clear about what has taken place and what has been agreed to.

Communicating

Telephone Skills

$\mathcal{T}$he cost of calling long distance is decreasing and more call centres are springing up to deal with customer sales, help, and inquiries. People in these centres are trained to satisfy customers. As a consequence, customer expectations are high, and rising. Here are some ideas of how you can excel on the phone.

1. Greet people warmly. Let people know immediately that you are there to serve. Start off with an introduction such as "This is John Day speaking. How may I help you?"

2. Have a purpose in mind. Focus on it to reduce time on unrelated issues.

3. Use your time effectively by stating your purpose and getting agreement to it. If you are calling someone, ask if this is a good time for him.

4. Use the person's name whenever possible. It shows interest and respect. Don't use a first name unless you have asked for permission to do so. If the other person uses your first name, you are probably at liberty to do so in return.

5. Avoid any signs of a lack of interest in the call, such as
- carrying on a second conversation;
- working on your computer simultaneously;
- delivering a standard greeting, especially when delivered in a monotone;
- chewing gum or eating while talking.

6. Listen to what people are telling you. As you can't see people and respond to their non-verbal body language, listen for hesitation and pauses. Follow up with probing questions such as "I don't detect that you are sure. Is that so? Can you tell me why?"

7. Emphasize key messages. Your voice will need to do the selling for you. Raise your voice and enunciate key ideas by speaking slower at critical points in the conversation.

8. Keep your tone positive. Judging from your voice, clients should never be in any doubt that you want to help them.

9. Don't put people on hold unless it's absolutely necessary. If you need to do so, ask for their permission first. Also, let them know approximately how long they may need to wait. When you come back, greet them by name and thank them for holding.

10. Avoid jargon. Every company develops its own language, which probably is not known to people on the outside. Make it easy for people to understand you by using everyday language whenever possible.

11. When speaking to clients, demonstrate their value to your business. Complete the call by thanking them for calling, or for their time and/or business.

12. Help solve the problem. The process begins by defining the problem clearly. This is best done by asking the 5 *W*s and an *H*: *Who* is responsible, *what* happened, *when* did it happen, *where* did it take place, *why* did it happen, and *how* did happen? When you are done, help the client define the problem clearly by summarizing the issue succinctly.

Communicating

In a Virtual Environment

$\mathcal{I}$n a global economy, people who are located in different cities and countries often work together on common projects. Some of the team players work for the organization while others are contractors. All should be seen as partners in the process. Here are some ideas as to how to work effectively together:

1. *Voice mail.* Set up a system to allow people to call in their results to a central number. This data can be updated regularly and fed back to all interested parties.

2. *Teleconferencing.* The cost of meeting with people out of town is high, so teleconferencing has become the cheaper alternative. It is possible to set up a number and have all members of the meeting call in at a specified time.

3. *Internet meetings.* While the technology is far from perfect, it is possible to hold a meeting on the Internet. NetMeetings (Microsoft), for example, allows people to communicate on a split screen so that typed messages go back and forth. It is also possible to draw on a board and have the other person see it as it is being done. Finally, it is possible to see each other with the use of a relatively inexpensive camera perched on your desk.

4. *Self-directed learning.* People needing to learn similar skills can do so on an as-needed basis by accessing increasingly popular tele-classes. While this form of learning is not always ideal, it can provide a low-cost alternative to classroom training for certain skills.

5. *E-mail.* This is quickly taking the place of conventional mail as the best and cheapest form of communication. E-mail saves paper and stamps, is typically easy to do, and can be sent with attachments, including voice messages.

6. *Pagers and cellular phones.* New satellite technologies are enabling people to stay in touch anywhere in the world — at a cost. Within a country, it is easy and inexpensive to update people on a daily basis.

7. *Chat-lines on the Internet or an intranet.* Organizations can encourage communications by setting up bulletin boards where people can post questions and get answers. Useful information for others on the team can be posted there too.

8. *Project management.* People sharing the same software can track their progress simultaneously to ensure that they are on time and within budget.

9. *Sharing a common vision and goal.* If everyone is aware of and buying into a common vision, they will all be marching in the same direction. If they have established the goal of the project together, they will be committed to achieving it.

Communicating

With Peers

A well-informed employee is the best sales person a company can have.

E. J. THOMAS

Teamwork is really important in the workplace. Working co-operatively for the benefit of the customers is the purpose of your job. You will enjoy your job much more if the atmosphere is collaborative and positive. This will depend largely on how people communicate with each other. Be the role model, and use these principles to improve communication with and among your peers:

1. Become a better receiver of information and facilitate upward communication. Employees need to feel they have a chance to influence what goes on in your organization. Use these communication principles with both peers and subordinates to encourage a free exchange of ideas.

2. Encourage opinions from other people. Listen to all ideas before formulating your own.

3. Show your peers that you respect their ideas by encouraging them to contribute and listening to what they have to say.

4. If you are at all confused about an idea being presented, try repeating it in your own words. This will not only clarify your understanding, but will also show you are interested.

5. Really listen to your colleagues — don't just wait to jump in with your own ideas. Listen to their words, thoughts, and feelings.

6. Ask for opinions from both peers and subordinates. This makes them feel that their contributions are valued, and will give them a greater sense of commitment.

7. Support your colleagues' ideas even when they differ from your own. You will be rewarded when you need support for your ideas.

8. Express your ideas in plain language. Confusing people with big words or jargon is not going to get your message across.

9. Use words carefully. Your listeners may react negatively to words that you thought were neutral. For example, using "you" when attributing blame will put associates on the defensive. Using "I" will build interest in your feedback. For example, "I am concerned" is preferable to "you did."

10. If you have to communicate bad news, do so privately. An informal one-on-one meeting will soften the blow, give your colleague an opportunity to express her feelings, and open the way to solving problems.

11. Be aware of how you communicate. Avoid alienating your colleagues by
- preaching (you are implying they are less morally responsible than you);
- patronizing (you are treating them like children);
- scolding (you are putting them down);
- being negative (you are always looking for the flaws).

12. Focus on the problem, not the person. Take a neutral approach to new ideas, then, after you have judged them, point out their positive aspects first. You want to encourage your colleagues to keep on thinking and contributing.

13. Act positively towards new ideas. Smile and show interest as they are being presented.

14. Don't use criticism of your boss as a way to win over your colleagues — you will be demonstrating that you can't be trusted when people's backs are turned.

15. If you don't agree with your boss's directions to others, keep it to yourself. Express your concerns to your boss, not to your colleagues.

16. If your fellow workers are angry with you,
- avoid arguments — they make things worse;
- listen to their concerns — they will feel better after venting their frustrations;
- acknowledge their right to feel angry;
- get their ideas on how to solve the problem.

Communicating

With Management

Communication is the key to

success . . . pass it on.

MAXWELL MALTZ

$\mathcal{I}$f you want to do your job well, you have to be able to communicate effectively with your superiors. This skill is particularly important for career advancement.

1. Make sure your boss knows what is happening, especially if there are problems. Bosses need to be prepared for difficult situations — put yourself in their shoes, and don't give them an opportunity to blame you for embarrassing them.

2. Be prompt with bad news. If your boss first hears about problems through office gossip, your version of the situation will sound weak and defensive.

3. If you have an urgent matter to deal with, set up a meeting with your boss to talk about it. When you make the appointment, let her know the subject of the meeting and how long it should take.

4. If your knowledge and advice are creating positive effects, make sure management is aware of this.

5. If you are presenting an idea, have written backup material on hand whenever possible. Your documentation will continue to sell the idea after your presentation is over.

6. Present ideas clearly and briefly. Bosses are busy people, and over-explaining will weaken your case.

7. Project confidence in your ideas and your information. Speak firmly, and reinforce your argument with body language. Emphasize critical points by leaning forward and making eye contact with your audience.

8. Highlight solutions, not problems. Let your bosses know that you have the answers and are willing to implement them.

9. Use language carefully. Avoid phrases that suggest the opposite of what you intend. For example, "To tell the truth" suggests you haven't been honest up to that point. Try not to use overheated expressions such as "awful news" rather than "important information."

10. Resist the urge to show anger or to avoid your boss when you are having a disagreement. Let your emotions cool down, and then calmly present your view of the issue, explaining the reason for your opinions. Use "I" statements to avoid sounding aggressive. For example, you could say, "I don't think this is fair," rather than "You're being unreasonable."

11. Accept criticism from your boss as feedback. Turn criticism into a learning session by asking what your boss's response would be to a similar situation.

12. If you would like to introduce an important new idea to your workplace but are not sure how it will be received, first mention it to your boss in writing. This will give you a chance to explain the issue as you would like, and will also allow your boss time to think about it.

13. Don't go over your boss's head, unless there is absolutely no alternative. If you must, make sure you inform your boss first.

Communicating

The Ten Deadly Sins

*The most practical advice for leaders
is not to treat pawns like pawns, nor princes like princes,
but all persons like persons.*

JAMES MACGREGOR BURNS

Here is a list of things to avoid when dealing with others:

1. *Being patronizing.* This is praising people when it is clearly unwarranted, or using a tone of voice that suggests that the individual is a lot better than he or she in fact is.

2. *Using generalities.* Examples include: "You have a bad attitude," or "Your work is seldom satisfactory."

3. *Using labels to describe a person.* Examples include phrases such as "You're paranoid," or "Your behaviour is neurotic." Playing psychologist belittles others and does nothing to solve the problem.

4. *Being sarcastic.* This is an indirect way of dealing with a problem. It's better to be more direct.

5. *Telling people to do something instead of asking them to.* People don't respond to being treated like children.

6. *Railroading.* Using a position of power, fast pace, or poor logic to bully people into accepting something.

7. *Threatening. Giving a person an ultimatum.* Explaining why you want something done will always work better, especially if you want to maintain a long-term relationship. Threatening is sometimes appropriate with someone you are never likely to deal with again, but even then should be used only as a last resort.

8. *Giving advice before being asked.* If you have an idea for someone, ask them if they would be interested.

9. *Being vague.* Be specific. Give examples. Tell your listener what happened, when and where it happened, and how often.

10. *Exaggerating.* Using words such as "always" or "never" might confirm that there is a problem, but it makes the problem seem far worse than it actually is. As a result, you will annoy people and cause them to reject your idea or request.

Conflict

Prevention

*A fault is a crack, gradually widening
and separating people.*

CARL JUNG

Preventing a conflict from happening is much better than having to deal
with one that has occurred. Here's how to avoid conflict and maintain
harmonious relationships with co-workers:

1. Avoid being continuously judgemental of others. Judge them by
their actions and results, rather than by who they are.

2. Stop trying to change people. Try to influence their actions and
behaviour, because you will not be able to change their personalities.

3. Be helpful to others whenever possible. When they are overloaded,
offer to assist. You'll earn the gratitude of those around you.

4. When people are angry at you or at others, give them a chance to
blow off steam without interruption. You don't have to agree with
their point of view, but you can agree with their right to be angry.

5. Listen to others. Give people a chance to influence you without cutting them off or developing a rebuttal before they have even finished expressing their idea.

6. Maintain a cheerful disposition. It is hard for people to pick an argument with someone who has a positive demeanour.

7. Keep the lines of communication open. Always be open to the opinions and ideas of others.

8. Make humour a part of the workplace. Keep things light. It will never be taken as a sign that you don't care.

9. Focus on facts and information, rather than on rumours and feelings.

10. Involve people in changes that you make. Listen to and understand their interests, objectives, and concerns.

11. Deal with issues that are hard to discuss, otherwise the problem will intensify. Understand why these "undiscussables" exist, so they can be brought to the surface and dealt with.

12. Immediately resolve issues that prevent completion of obligations by the targeted date.

13. Don't shy away from conflict about ideas. Point out that you respect the opinions of others, even though you may not agree with them.

14. Develop an understanding with your colleagues as to how conflict will be dealt with when it arises.

15. Keep your ear to the ground. Tap into the grapevine so that you can identify issues before they get blown out of proportion. Deal with these issues before they become disruptive.

16. Participate in setting ground rules for your team. Reiterate, for example, that members don't have to like each other, but they should respect each other.

Conflict

Between You and Others

If your neighbour does you some harm,
do not pretend you are still friends. . . . Do not hate him,
but reprove him for what he did and through this
peace can be re-established.

RASHBAM, BIBLICAL SCHOLAR

Conflict about ideas is good. It creates new opportunities to explore options that can lead to improvement. But conflict between people is harmful. It creates tension, ill health, and a diversion away from the daily task of customer service. Here are some strategies for dealing with this problem quickly and professionally:

BEFORE YOU TAKE ACTION

1.
- Evaluate your ability to resolve the issue. If this is something you have difficulty with, as most people do, seek the advice of someone you trust. Perhaps he will do a role-play with you to hone your skill at handling the situation.
- Deal quickly with personality conflict so that the problem doesn't mushroom or become a situation you condone.
- Ask the person with whom you have a "beef" for permission to

deal with the issue. Simply approach him and say, "Could the two of us sit down and discuss our differences? I'd really like to do that." An acceptance will set the climate for a collaborative, adult-to-adult problem-solving session.

- Find a neutral venue where your colleagues cannot observe you.
- Collect your thoughts so you are well prepared. Make some notes so you don't forget what you intend to say.

AT THE MEETING

2.
- Thank the other person for working with you to solve your differences.
- Establish the climate for a good interchange. Be constructive and positive in your words, voice tone, and body language. Point out that the conflict is not good for either of you, and that you are determined to resolve it.
- Make the point that there are two sides to every story, and that you are probably the source of the problem too.
- Invite the other person to state the issues first. If he does, do not interrupt. Take notes if necessary. Listen to what she is saying and how she is saying it.
- Summarize the other person's points to show that you understand. Show empathy. A statement such as "I would feel like that too" will go a long way to reducing the anger, so you can both get on with solving the problem.
- If the other person declines to state the problem, state your case. Be firm and clear. Maintain eye contact.
- Be specific about the things that bother you. Don't assume that the other person knows what you are thinking or feeling.
- Give examples of the things that upset you. Don't exaggerate or stretch the truth. Avoid using the words "never" and "always."
- Don't use inflammatory language. If you do, the person will

respond to your anger rather than to the content of your message.

- Avoid labels that tend to simplify the issue. Phrases such as "women do that" will increase the emotion and tension, and will prevent a rational discussion of the issues.

- Be assertive. Use "I" statements instead of "you" statements. Phrases such as "I feel angry" are more likely to encourage the other person to want to offer a solution than "you" statements. Comments such as "You did this or that" will tend to make the other person defensive.

- Don't go back in history. Stick to current events.

- Once you both agree on the problem, move on to solutions. Offer ideas about what you will do to address his concerns. Then you can ask what he will do to address your issues. Involving your colleague in problem-solving will increase his commitment to resolving the problem.

- Agree to disagree where no resolution can be found. Indicate your respect for the other person's position even if you do not agree with it. But don't give up without trying creative ways of solving each other's problems. Keep looking for creative solutions by using "what if?" statements. Call a time-out if necessary. Some issues are difficult to resolve in one session. Consider taking a break and revisiting the issues with new perspectives.

- Conclude the meeting with a summary of your discussions.

AFTERWARDS

3.
- Be mindful of issues raised at your meeting. Live up to commitments, and express appreciation if others live up to theirs.

- If the issue is not resolved, consider inviting a third party to intervene on your behalf.

Conflict

Mediation

It's better to debate a question without settling it,
than to settle a question without debating it.

JOSEPH JOUBERT

Organizations today are using empowered teams to deliver services better, cheaper, and faster than those in traditional hierarchical workplaces. In such environments, people are more responsible for everything, including their relationships with each other. With traditional managers fast disappearing, you can expect to be called upon to mediate differences that emerge between your associates. This will challenge your interpersonal skills, sense of fairness, and patience. These guidelines will reduce the possibility of the problem "exploding" in front of you.

BEFORE A MEDIATION MEETING

1. Determine whether the conflict is serious enough to warrant action. A serious conflict is one that affects the morale of the team and its ability to serve its customers.

2. Evaluate whether your associates are able to solve the problem themselves. If they have the maturity and experience to resolve the

matter on their own, encourage them to do so. Make sure you
follow up on the matter. If it has been suitably dealt with,
compliment your colleagues.

3. If the problem is disrupting team performance and the associates
involved are unable to solve it on their own, set up a meeting at
which both people will be present.

4. In your planning for the meeting, gain an understanding of the
issues by establishing the nature of each person's problem. Are
the issues real or are they simply misunderstandings?

5. Prepare a meeting room in which you have two chairs facing a flip
chart or chalkboard. Your chair can face the two combatants.

AT A MEDIATION MEETING

6. • Confirm that both associates have agreed to your mediation.
   • Describe your role as mediator. Indicate that you will not take
     sides. By remaining neutral, you will help the parties produce
     an outcome that satisfies both of them.
   • Go over the background information. Keep the tone positive.
     Establish and get agreement on the goal for which you want
     each person to strive. Say, for example, "By the end of our
     meeting we want to —. Do you agree to help meet that
     objective?"
   • Establish rules for the meeting. Each person should
     — show respect for the other's ideas;
     — try to see the other person's viewpoint;
     — focus on the problem, not on the other person;
     — look for commonalities rather than differences;
     — make an effort to find a solution.

7. Review in a non-threatening manner what will happen if the problem remains unsolved. For example, you can say, "If we don't solve the problem, the tension will continue to increase and will affect our service. I will then be forced to impose a solution — something I am reluctant to do."

8. Use humour to relieve tension. For example, try exaggerating the problem to help your colleagues put it into perspective.

9. Ask the combatants to state their positions as objectively as possible, and then summarize in your own words to aid understanding. Help the parties prioritize the issues, focusing on the important points. List each person's key issues on the flip chart to aid objective consideration.

10. Deal with the most important issues first, alternating between the two lists, to get to the root of the problem. Ask for suggestions; if your colleagues have none, start with some of your own. When you discover the cause (or causes) of the problem, summarize and confirm agreement with your colleagues.

11. Once the cause has been determined, focus on solutions. Get each party to come up with solutions and dates by which they will be implemented.

12. At the end of the meeting, summarize the discussion so everyone will be clear about the cause of the problem and how it is to be resolved. Thank your colleagues for their co-operation, praising them if they have shown openness and taken chances.

13. • Set up a progress-review meeting. If the situation has improved, praise your colleagues and offer your continued support. If things are much as they were, find the cause and keep working with the parties until they can reach a friendly solution.

• If one or both of the parties refuses to co-operate in resolving the situation, and your team's performance is being compromised, you should recommend disciplinary action.

Counselling Interview

Don't fret if the temptation to give advice is overwhelming,
because the tendency to ignore it is universal.

UNKNOWN

𝒥rom time to time, your performance may not meet the expectations of your boss and you could be made aware of your shortcomings. It is better that this is done informally at your workstation or more formally in your boss's office. This is preferable to having poor performance documented and kept in your file, as may happen in a performance appraisal or, worse still, a disciplinary interview. If your boss asks you to discuss her concerns with your performance, here is how you can turn a potentially negative situation into a positive one:

BEFORE THE DISCUSSION

1.
- Ask for a little time to prepare.
- Take time to cool down. Being angry or defensive will just exacerbate the situation.
- Collect any facts that may have relevance — the number of mistakes, customer complaints, etc.

- Review any goals your boss has set for you. Have you met those expectations or fallen short of them?
- Be open-minded about what your boss has to say. Be prepared to listen and learn. If your performance has not met the standards and expectations, think about how you can improve. Prepare a plan for change.
- Take notepaper to the meeting.

DURING THE DISCUSSION

2.
- Be courteous. Greet your boss with a smile. This will help set the climate for problem-solving rather than confrontation.
- Listen to the problem as described by your boss. Make notes if necessary.
- Show your agreement to any facts presented. Where opinions are presented, think about them before responding.
- Indicate to your boss that you are there to solve the problem, and that you appreciate the feedback you are being given. For you, this is an opportunity to learn and improve.
- If your boss is being vague, ask for specifics. In a collaborative tone of voice, say things like: "Hmmm, can you give me an example of that?" or "Gee, I can't think of having done that. Can you remind me of that occurrence?"
- Get involved in developing a plan for improvement. Separate the things you will do from those with which you may need help. For example, you may
  - try harder;
  - be more careful;
  - be more courteous;
  - need more training;
  - need documented standards or procedures.

- Ask for your boss's assistance if you feel that he has
  - not coached you;
  - failed to give you regular feedback;
  - not acknowledged your successes;
  - not set goals.
- Many people don't have goals that are SMART (Specific, Measurable, Agreed upon, Realistic, Time-based). If this is the case with you, ask your boss if you can negotiate some short- and medium-term goals. Write down what was agreed upon.
- Confirm that your boss has agreed to help you by asking an open-ended question, such as "Can you help me by describing what we have agreed to, so that I am really clear about it all?"
- Summarize your understanding of everything said to make sure that all expectations are clear.
- Thank your boss for the opportunity to be involved in finding ways of improving performance. Ask her to always be frank with you if she is not satisfied.
- Leave with a handshake.

AFTER THE DISCUSSION

3.
- Follow up meticulously on everything agreed upon with your boss.
- After a month, ask for feedback if it has not already been given, so you are assured that your performance is on track.

Creativity

Behold the turtle! He makes progress only
when he sticks his neck out.

ANONYMOUS

Only by venturing out into the unknown do we enable
new ideas and new results to take shape.

MARGARET WHEATLEY

The future of your organization will, in large measure, be determined by your ability to innovate and change. The creative process, if properly employed, will allow you to move ahead — perhaps in quantum leaps. Here are some strategies you can use to become more creative yourself and encourage those around you to do so too.

1. Look for new ideas constantly. Search the Internet, read books and magazines, attend exhibitions and workshops.

2. Keep your mind open to ideas from unexpected places. Allow your mind to wander, especially in places you do not normally visit. Keep a pen and pad to jot down new ideas.

3. If you work with critical people, keep your ideas to yourself until you have had a chance to formulate them fully. With each idea, think about the benefits, drawbacks, and costs. Anticipate and find solutions to possible objections.

4. Don't exclude any ideas by deciding in advance whether others will accept them. Concern yourself with selling the idea only as a last step. If you try to sell it before you're ready, you may inhibit your imagination and creativity.

5. Don't always expect to get home runs. Look for small improvements rather than major breakthroughs. Don't put undue pressure on yourself. As you become more innovative and your confidence grows, so will the size of your ideas.

6. Ask your boss for a budget for some level of experimentation, including time and materials. This will send a strong signal to you and your colleagues about the importance the company places on innovation.

7. Permit yourself to make mistakes. Consider them a stepping stone on the way to success.

8. Be persistent. Sometimes the skeptics jump in quickly, especially if they know you will be easily discouraged. Stay with your idea if you are convinced of its value.

9. Be open to the ideas of others, and they will become more supportive of you too. Be open and responsive to new ideas. Listen to be influenced rather than concentrating on developing a rebuttal.

10. If you find it difficult to assess the merits of your idea, find someone who can and who may become a spokesperson. Often it's not what you say but how you say it. Some people have a talent for being persuasive.

11. Encourage the boss to make tools of creativity freely available. A flip chart in your work area can be a place to post new ideas as they occur to people. People can also use Post-it Notes to jot down their ideas, and then leave them on the flip chart on the way to a break.

12. Look outside your department or organization for new ideas that could work for you. While you may get ideas from similar work areas within your organization, you will usually find more innovative solutions in other organizations and industries. These ideas can be found by
- reading trade journals;
- interviewing new employees who worked for an organization that had similar work processes;
- attending conferences and shows, where you can network with people from other organizations;
- getting information from your trade organization;
- scouring the Internet;
- using Internet chat features for sharing and researching new ideas.

13. At your departmental meetings, take a leadership role by challenging your colleagues to think more of reasons why a new idea would work, rather than reasons why it would not.

Creativity

Opportunities multiply as they are seized.

SUN TZU

To entrepreneurs and innovators, there is no such thing as failure. Failure is just an opportunity to do it again and do it smarter, because they know what doesn't work.

CHIPS KLEIN

The process most commonly used to encourage creativity, brainstorming, works only in a group situation. Another process that can be used both individually and in a team environment is the SCAMPER process. The process works particularly well in creating new products and services that will add additional value to customers. Here is how to use the SCAMPER process, step by step:

SUBSTITUTE

1. Think of ways of replacing one thing with another. For example, could plastic replace wood, aluminum, or steel? Could electronic transfer replace the mail or a phone call replace a fax message?

COMBINE

2. Are there ways of bringing things together that could result in one unique item? For example, could some services be combined to produce one-stop shopping?

ADJUST, ADD, OR ADAPT

3. Figure out what changes can be made to improve products. Similar products could be added together, for example, such as two blades joined to a twin razor. Adding stamps to each other can create a single roll or sheet. An alternative is to unite dissimilar products to create something new, such as a Swiss Army knife.

MODIFY, MAGNIFY, OR MINIATURIZE

4. Think about the possibilities of changing the size or the nature of the product itself. Post-it Notes have done an exceptional job of taking the basic technology of a multiple-stick product and producing different sizes, colours, shapes, and uses.

PUT PRODUCTS TO OTHER USES

5. This is a commonly used strategy. Excess newspapers can be made into fire logs; a kitchen knife can be used as a screwdriver.

ELIMINATE OR ELABORATE

6. Consider the benefits that can be derived from less use. For example, packaging is reduced if refills are used. Generic products save advertising.

7. Investigate the advantages of changing the order or sequence of events, or see if things can work the opposite way. One example with a twist on this theme would be a car that goes in two directions, not only one.

Customer Service

If we don't take care of the customer . . . someone else will.

ANONYMOUS

W hether you're in the private or public sector, your very existence will ultimately depend on whether you meet the needs of the customer. This is not always understood in the public sector, where customers are sometimes taken for granted. Increasingly, departments that are failing to live up to the expectations of customers are finding themselves downsized and their services outsourced to the private sector, where accountability seems to be greater. Here are some very important facts to bear in mind in considering the quality of the services you currently provide:

1. Build relationships with customers. Word-of-mouth advertising is far more effective than other forms. Promote word of mouth by exceeding people's expectations at every opportunity.

2. Always strive for exceptional service. Always focus on how you and your teammates can meet customers' needs.

3. Make customer issues the highest priority in your team meetings.

4. Invite customers to visit your workplace. Ask them how they think you are doing.

- What do they like?
- What would they like to see change?
- Do other service providers provide other or better services?

5. Remind yourself and your colleagues about the importance of customers by displaying visual cues around the workplace. Post your mission statement, a document outlining what your purpose is; who your customers are; where you operate; how you serve customers; why you do what you do.

6. Determine what is important for customer satisfaction, such as promptness and quality of service. Display these indicators to remind yourself of the importance of your customers.

7. Collect data on your team's service performance to encourage your colleagues' sense of responsibility.

8. Ask your customers for feedback on the effectiveness of your service. Use written surveys or personal interviews, analyze the data, and determine what your priorities should be. Get your whole team to participate in making suggestions for and implementing change.

9. Help create a positive environment for your colleagues, since the best guarantee of great service is high morale among your team members. They will feel encouraged if they are listened to, kept informed, and recognized for achievement.

10. Find out about, and make sure everyone knows, your organization's minimum standards for customer service. And make sure your colleagues know *why* these standards are important.

11. Celebrate improvements in customer service. If performance is slipping, let the team members know, and solicit their ideas for making positive changes.

12. Improve customer service by learning how to handle difficult customers; how to listen; what customers want; how to solve customer problems; telephone skills.

13. Clarify the level of power you and your team members have to make necessary decisions. Ensure that your team has guidelines and training that will equip it to solve customer problems quickly and effectively.

14. Seek from your boss the authority you need to solve customer problems. Once you have proved that you can use this responsibility wisely and effectively, ask for increased power to act on your own.

15. Treat angry customers with empathy. Viewing the situation from the customer's perspective will increase your enthusiasm for dealing with problems without focusing on the customer's behaviour.

16. Give your home phone number to customers, but only when this action will not be misunderstood. Show them you care by encouraging them to call if they need help outside business hours.

17. Encourage people in your team to benchmark the team's effectiveness. Compare your procedures and performance with those of other departments and organizations involved in similar activities. You can learn a great deal from this process, especially when the other group is very different from your own.

Decision-Making

With Your Teammates

*Nothing is more difficult, and therefore more precious,
than to be able to decide.*

NAPOLEON BONAPARTE

How decisions are made has a lot to do with how effective the decisions turn out to be.

1. There are many ways to make decisions with your team. Most commonly, decisions can be made by
- one person, such as your boss, or a few people (minority);
- most of your teammates (majority);
- the support of everyone (consensus).

2. Appreciate that you cannot be involved in every decision, nor should you be. Minority decisions should be made when
- there is an emergency;
- time does not permit any discussion;
- health and safety are issues;
- you have an expert on your team who is best qualified to deal with that issue.

3. The support of the majority of people is an effective decision-making process when

- a decision is required quickly;
- there are too many people to negotiate a consensus;
- the issue is very divisive.

4. Decisions that impact your entire team should be made by consensus.

5. If your team members want to reach a consensus, let them know the place and time for the meeting in advance. With a few days' notice, they will have time to consider alternative ideas and arrive at the meeting having made an informed choice.

6. Invite a facilitator to help you through the process. Alternatively, one of the team members can take this neutral role.

7. At the meeting, the team can reach consensus quickly using the nominal group technique. This technique consists of eight steps. The facilitator should:

- *Set a goal.* "We want to reach consensus on finding the [pick a number] best . . . "
- *Get agreement to the process.* Ask participants if they will support the majority. Any other constraints should also be agreed to.
- *Allow people to collect their thoughts and ideas.* Participants record their ideas on a piece of paper.
- *Collect ideas by round robin.* Team members take turns stating their ideas. These ideas are recorded on the flip chart without discussion.
- *Clarify and lobby.* Evaluate key ideas in greater detail. If you

have a long list, vote to establish the top five. Allow time for people to express their support for ideas, finding out why they feel the way they do.

- *Take a vote.* Participants make their choices and the choices are assigned a score. For example, first choice gets five points, second choice gets three points, third choice gets one point. Alternatively, members can vote on all items that they consider significant.
- *Tally the votes.* Count the votes for each idea and identify the top choice(s).
- *Check for consensus.* Check to see if everyone agrees with the majority or at least supports the most popular choice.

8. If the team cannot reach a consensus, you may
- look for a compromise;
- review the top two or three issues and revote.

9. If rigidity persists, you might pass the decision to your boss. Generally, people will find this acceptable when they did have a chance to reach a consensus first.

Decision-Making

Individual

Do or do not. There is no try.

YODA, FROM THE MOVIE *THE EMPIRE STRIKES BACK*

We are all faced with many choices every day. Some are easy and others are tough. Dealing successfully with the tough issues is a skill that will reduce stress and save time. Here is a step-by-step process that will help.

LOOK AT ALL YOUR OPTIONS

1. If the problem is large, important, or complex, write it down. If not, visualize each alternative. Don't exclude any options, no matter how crazy they may seem.

EVALUATE YOUR CHOICES LOGICALLY

2. Think of the pros and cons of each option. Weight according to criteria such as speed of implementation, simplicity, and cost. Give a score to each and figure out which option scores highest overall.

EVALUATE EACH CHOICE INTUITIVELY

3. • Which "feels" better? Which best fits with your values and morals? If you are not sure, try flipping a coin. If the choice is one that feels right, go with it. If it feels wrong, then you know that the other option is probably better.
   • Alternative techniques of evaluation include asking a trusted friend or mentor. Listen to his or her advice without negating choices.
   • Construct a decision tree. With each option, you create two branches — a yes and a no branch. Keep the yes branch progressing until you reach a solution.

MAKE THE DECISION

4. Make it boldly and with conviction, because it will prove to be the right decision only if you make it so. You owe it to yourself to make your choice successful.

DEVELOP AN ACTION PLAN

5. List the steps necessary to complete the decision successfully. Carry them out until you have proven to yourself that the decision was a good one.

Delegation

$\mathcal{T}$he best executives are those that have the sense to pick good people. With an increased emphasis on teamwork, you will be called upon to co-operate and share the workload. From time to time, you can ask someone to assist by taking on an activity that you have done up to this point. In this section we discuss what you should delegate, to whom, and how the delegated task should be done.

WHAT

1. You simply cannot do everything, be everywhere, and control all decisions. Give your colleagues credit for being able to cope with some of your less demanding tasks.

2. Clear any ideas about delegation beforehand with your boss.

3. Document your activities for a week. Divide tasks into two categories: those that only you can do and those that can be delegated. Here are some examples of the latter group:
- routine jobs;
- collecting data;
- attending routine meetings unrelated to your major tasks.

4. Decide who would be suitable to help you reduce your workload. Consider

- their interest in the tasks;
- their available time;
- their skill levels.

5. If you identify people who have the time and interest but not the appropriate skills, offer to train them in the new tasks.

6. Meet formally or informally, as the situation dictates, with the people to whom tasks will be delegated.

- Explain the purpose of the meeting.
- Describe the task that needs doing.
- Confirm the goal(s) of the task, making sure the delegate agrees.
- Agree on a completion date.
- Make clear the importance of prompt and accurate performance.
- Divide large projects into a series of mini-goals with their own timelines.
- Don't forget to stress the benefits of the new responsibility. These might include enhanced status, opportunities to learn, exposure within the company, or a chance for promotion.
- Make sure the delegate is aware of, and accepts the scope of, the task and the duties involved. Indicate your mutual agreement with a handshake.

7. Hand over responsibility and authority along with the task. Indicate to all concerned that you have confidence in the delegate's ability.

8. Encourage the delegate to bring up any concerns or doubts about the task before beginning, and help solve them before they become problems.

9. Monitor performance to make sure your directions have been understood.

10. Continue monitoring with decreasing frequency as the delegate becomes familiar with the task. Give positive feedback for a good performance and helpful, uncritical advice if there are problems.

11. Give delegates enough room to carry out new responsibilities in their own style, if appropriate.

12. Let your boss and other colleagues know that you have delegated the task and to whom, and that your delegate has the authority to carry it through. You, however, bear the ultimate responsibility for the success or failure of the delegation.

Difficult People
How to Handle Them

*God grant me the serenity to accept the things I cannot change,
the courage to change the things I can, and the ability to
hide the bodies of the people that really tick me off!*

UNKNOWN

*L*ife is about making choices. You can choose the people you want to befriend. But sometimes, in a work situation, you may not be able to avoid people who make your stomach turn when you see them.

1. The type of people you want as little to do with as possible are people who

- enjoy your failures;
- insist on telling you what to do without giving you an opportunity to make your own decisions;
- interrupt at meetings;
- show no respect for others or their opinions;
- always discuss others in non-complimentary terms behind their backs;
- try to take credit when they have made little or no contribution to a project;

- find it hard to tell the truth;
- compete when they should be collaborating.

2. Here are some strategies for dealing with such people:
   - Learn to live with them. Despite all the bad faults some people may have, they're bound to have some good qualities. Find out what they are and focus on them.
   - Work around them. Go out of your way to avoid such people. Send them notes, faxes, or e-mails instead of phoning or getting into face-to-face conversations. This will work particularly well if the person in question will be around for only a short while.
   - Focus on the issues. Try not to criticize them, for to do so will only increase your frustration as their behaviour deteriorates.
   - If you can bear it no more, let the person know how he affects you. This can be very delicate, so do so with great caution. The principles of giving feedback (*see* Feedback: Giving) will help you do this in a way that will reduce rather than exacerbate the problem.
   - Do some self-examination. Become introspective. Ask yourself if you are perfect. The answer will surely be no. It could be that things you do annoy others. Work to improve yourself and change your behaviour. As you do, you will surely see an improvement in the behaviour of others.
   - Find some common ground with the person you don't like. This will help you build bridges and give you things to talk about. As you get to know the person better, you may find out things that will give you some insight into why she behaves as she does.
   - Treat difficult people with respect. You set the tone. You behave professionally. Doing so will, at a minimum, prevent your relationship from deteriorating. And at least you will have the satisfaction of doing what you expect of others.

Disciplinary Interview

The superior man always remembers how he was punished.
The inferior man always remembers what presents he got.

CONFUCIUS

*H*aving a disciplinary interview is an unpleasant experience for both you and your boss. Needless to say, you should always strive to perform at a level that will earn you accolades, not rebukes. In the event that you are asked to participate in this process, here are some things you can do:

BEFORE THE INTERVIEW

1.
- Prepare yourself thoroughly. You will obviously know the reason for the interview. Collect whatever facts you can, particularly those that may be in your favour.
- Prepare mentally. Do not go in looking for a fight. Plan to come out of the process better and wiser. Be prepared to learn and find ways of improving yourself, but also be prepared to defend yourself should the process be unfair.
- If you work in a unionized workplace, inform your shop steward of the interview, although the company probably will already have done this. Find out what rights you have or don't have.

2.
- Respond to reason, logic, and the facts.
- Listen to what is being said. Don't be defensive. Make notes. Ask for clarification and specifics, particularly if your boss uses the words "always" and "never."
- Respond unemotionally, as difficult as that may seem. Focus on solutions. If you have difficulty coming up with a solution, ask your boss what he or she would do in your situation.
- Don't attack your boss unless you have ample reason to do so. If you do attack, focus on the issue rather than the person. Saying *"I* am aware of the following situations that have not been dealt with" is better than saying *"You* play favourites."
- Leave the meeting with a clear understanding of what is expected of you and a level of comfort that this can be done. If not, you should get whatever help is available to turn the situation around. This could include additional training or better equipment.

Diversity

Few people can be happy unless they hate
some other person, nation or creed.

BERTRAND RUSSELL

The workplace has become a melting pot for people of different cultures. Understanding and appreciating the diversity will become a source of motivation and enjoyment for you. Failing to respect other people's differences will lead to hostility, tension, and unhappiness. Here are some things you can do to take advantage of working in a multicultural environment:

1. Avoid offensive terms when referring to race, gender, or ethno-cultural background.

2. Team new employees, if possible, with partners from similar backgrounds until they find a place in your organization's culture.

3. Learn about the ethno-cultural backgrounds of people in your organization. You will discover useful information about
  • how to greet them;

- their sense of personal space;
- acceptable gestures;
- their cultures' attitudes towards authority and gender roles;
- compatible personality types;
- how they perceive time and the importance of punctuality;
- possible tensions with other nationalities;
- forms of humour;
- expression of emotions;
- views on what confers status.

4. Find out how long your associates from other cultures have been in the country. This knowledge will help you gauge their understanding of, and comfort with, local customs.

5. If you are working with people whose cultural attitudes towards time and punctuality differ from yours, bring up and discuss the difference, and try to negotiate a mutually acceptable solution.

6. Remember that different cultures have different degrees of comfort with physical closeness. What might appear standoffish to one person could seem a violation of personal space to another. Be careful about touching until you have a clear understanding of a person's distinction between friendly and offensive behaviours.

7. Find out the best way of communicating with each person. Some value directness and others find it rude. Some avoid asking questions because they consider it humiliating, so you must make extra efforts to ensure that they understand directions.

8. Under no circumstances should you tolerate racial slurs or other examples of prejudice in your workplace. Lack of action condones such behaviour. Make sure your colleagues understand that comments based on stereotypes are repugnant and unacceptable.

9. Support events that let staff members get together socially; these give them a chance to get to know each other better.

10. Use humour (avoiding stereotypes, of course) to promote a harmonious workplace. Show that you can laugh at your own mistakes, so your colleagues will feel at ease when they have to bring up disagreements.

11. Remember that your sense of humour may not seem funny to a person from another cultural group. Think about your audience before you make a joke.

12. Make special efforts to help people from minority groups achieve status in your organization. If you have a say in personnel matters, try to recruit, promote, and train people from other backgrounds so they are represented in all areas and levels of the workplace. Let them prove themselves by giving them increased responsibility and authority.

13. Spend more of your work and social time with people from backgrounds different from yours so you can get to know them better.

14. Pay attention to your body language when dealing with people from other ethno-cultural backgrounds, to avoid giving the wrong impression.

15. Be prepared for problems between your colleagues resulting from cultural conflict or misunderstanding. Deal with them as they arise, before they can turn into major crises.

16. Always try to adjust the work to fit the people, rather than expecting people to tailor their needs and cultural attitudes to the job.

17. Remember that cultural differences exist not only between people of different ethnic and religious backgrounds, but also between men and women, different age groups, and people of different sexual orientations.

Empowering

Giving Responsibility

The rung of a ladder was never meant to rest upon,
but only to hold a person's foot long enough to enable him
to put the other somewhat higher.

ALDOUS HUXLEY

The staff of an organization should be regarded as an asset to protect and develop, rather than a liability to decrease as much as possible. If you are in a supervisory position, you will find that you get the best results when you treat people as partners, increasing their level of authority as their skills and responsibilities increase. Here is what you can do:

1. Realize that you are not knowledgeable about everything, and that there is always an opportunity to learn from others — especially about the specifics of their particular jobs. Giving or sharing power is an act of generosity, courage, and leadership.

2. Assess each individual's willingness to be empowered. Each person has a different level of need. The best employees see the additional power as a vote of confidence and become increasingly motivated.

3. Avoid failure by assessing the person's ability to exercise the new power. Make sure that he is properly trained beforehand.

4. Make sure that people know the limits of their authority. When they show confidence and ability within those limits, consider increasing their power.

5. Give people a chance to find their own ways to attain objectives.

6. Don't fix other people's mistakes without first giving them a chance to do it themselves. They will learn to be responsible for their own decisions if they have an opportunity to learn from their own errors.

7. Monitor your management systems (decision-making, information flow, selection authority, accountability) frequently to make sure they encourage staff performance rather than present obstacles to it.

8. Increase the skills and confidence of your work group by making training an ongoing activity.

9. Follow this golden rule: treat other people as you would like to be treated. Develop personal relationships with your staff that are based on respect and trust.

10. If people are reluctant to assume new responsibilities, be patient. Try to make it clear to them that they, as well as you and the organization, will benefit from their increased effort and skills.

11. Be consistently supportive of your colleagues. As you win their trust, your people will be more willing to take on new challenges.

Empowerment

Taking Responsibility

There are two ways of exerting one's strength:
One is pushing down, the other is pulling up.

BOOKER T. WASHINGTON

*M*ost employees have found the concept of empowerment hollow and without meaning. While the idea raises the expectations of people to the possibilities of being treated like responsible adults, the reality is that most front-line people can't buy a three-hole punch for thirty-five dollars without approval. If your organization is proclaiming the new religion of empowerment, here's how you can benefit:

1. Meet with your boss. Ask him or her:
   - What will be different as a result of this new management philosophy. Press for specifics. If these are not forthcoming, provide some examples. "May I now settle clients' claims for up to one hundred dollars without authorization?"
   - To identify specific barriers that prevent more decisions being made at your level. If training is an issue, ask when the training might take place.
   - What the consequences are for mistakes.

2. If you are a team-based organization, there will be an expectation that you and your team will become increasingly self-managed. This presents exciting possibilities. You should encourage your team to meet to identify

- existing boundaries and parameters;
- new boundaries;
- increased responsibilities for such things as who will run team meetings, who will decide on allocating work, who will schedule holidays, who will deal with conflict, who will be responsible for hiring decisions, and how these decisions will be made.

3. If you are in a unionized organization and are part of the bargaining unit, you may be discouraged from doing things that are deemed to be managerial in nature. If you are in doubt, discuss the issue with your boss and your shop steward.

4. Some increased responsibilities may change the nature of your job. Your job classification could be impacted too, enabling you to earn more. If this is the case, consult your boss and people from human resources for advice.

Ethical and Moral Behaviour

Let unswerving integrity be your watchword.

BERNARD BARUCH

We make a living by what we get.
But we make a life by what we give.

WINSTON CHURCHILL

Behaving in an ethical manner is not only the right thing to do, but also a way of developing relationships that will yield significant dividends in the long term. Behaving morally also enables you to sleep well at night. Consider these ideas:

1. Avoid talking about people behind their backs, particularly if the comments are unflattering. Excuse yourself from any such discussions.

2. Tell the truth. It might hurt, but it can be coated in kindness. Saying "This work stinks" is far less effective than "There are two mistakes here that need to be corrected. Can you help me?"

3. Review your organization's values statement (if one is available). Try to tie your behaviour closely to those principles.

4. Don't spend time spying on people. Have them take responsibility for their own actions. Don't rat on them for petty transgressions — only if security and theft are involved.

5. If your peers do something you don't appreciate, point it out to them, not the boss. Be assertive and focus on the behaviour and not on the person.

6. Respect copyright. Everyone copies ideas, but copying entire workbooks and manuals deprives the creator of the royalties owed to them. If you do get ideas from others, give them credit. It will demonstrate your integrity publicly.

7. Be truthful. Keeping secrets and trying to be politically correct is stressful. Trying to behave as other people expect instead of being ourselves is denying our own right to feel good about who we are.

8. Don't make hasty assumptions based on how people appear. Make sure to get to know them before deciding if you want to establish a relationship.

9. Give credit where it's due. If, for example, you got help with a project that was particularly well received, let the people who dish out the brownie points know about those people who helped you. That way, you are demonstrating fairness. Equally important, you know you will be able to count on those same people when you need them in future.

10. Be careful not to lie on your resumé. If you get caught, it will cost you your job or a potential job, and it could put your career into a tailspin.

11. When dealing with colleagues, don't force your opinion on others by stating it as a fact. If you are stating it as a fact, back it up with data. If not, qualify your comment with "It's my opinion . . ."

12. Don't embarrass people publicly, especially your boss.

13. Don't send memos to your boss's boss unless you've cleared them in advance.

14. Copy your boss on memos sent outside your work area.

15. Don't make commitments you can't keep. Doing what you say you intend to do will
- energize you;
- enhance your reputation;
- save you time avoiding issues and people;
- enlarge your circle of like-minded and -acting people;
- keep your life simpler.

Etiquette
In the Office

Growing old is mandatory;
growing up is optional.

UNKNOWN

Behaving with courtesy and consideration for others helps to keep morale up so people can focus on real tasks instead of being angry at each other. Here are a few ideas to make life more pleasant in the office:

1. Don't jam the copier and then slide away.

2. Take out the coloured paper you were using in the copier and replace it with white paper.

3. Don't hog the fax machine.

4. Don't send forty-page faxes in prime time.

5. Make fresh coffee when it's your turn or you have had the last cup.

6. Don't leave your speaker phone on.

7. Don't get correction fluid on the copier glass.

8. Change the toner once in a while.

9. Treat other people's incoming faxes as important. Take them to the intended recipient right away.

10. Clean out the three-hole punch.

11. Close filing cabinet drawers when you're done.

12. Take your turn watering the office plants.

13. Don't send e-mail chain letters to your colleagues.

14. Keep your music low.

15. Encourage your office visitors to be respectful of others' space and privacy.

Exit Interview

*M*any organizations conduct exit interviews with people who have resigned. This is an excellent way of gathering information about problems in the organization. People leaving the organization are more likely to be frank than people who are staying, especially if the issue is about someone like a boss.

It's important that you leave on good terms with an employer in order to be able to use them as a reference for the future, so here are some tips on how to conduct yourself in the interview:

1. As an employee you should:
- Spend most of the time answering specific questions rather than volunteering information not asked for.
- Avoid using this as a venting session. Don't try to get back at people who upset you, but do be truthful.
- Confirm that the discussion is in confidence. Ask how the organization deals with the information. Based on that response, you can decide how important it is for you to disclose your information. The more serious the company is about changing things, the more forthcoming you might be.
- Deliver your message professionally. This means that you should:
  - Avoid foul language.

- Avoid exaggerating. Don't use words such as "never" or "always." Rather than "My boss never says good morning," say, "My boss isn't at her best in the mornings and doesn't greet me on some occasions."
- Give examples to back up your opinions. Say, "I'm not sure how committed the organization is to employee input, since neither one of my suggestions, submitted in writing, has been responded to." This is better than "Everyone knows that employees' opinions don't count around here."
- End on a positive note. Tell the interviewer about the positive things you found in the company. Let him know how you personally benefited from your experience.

2. If you are in a position of authority and are conducting an exit interview, the process will be more effective if you:
- Inform the exiting employee of your desire to collect information that could help improve working conditions.
- Ask if the associate prefers talking with you or someone else, such as a human-resources person.
- Ask the associate to discuss any issues that would be useful to you as a manager. Confirm that you will treat all information as confidential.
- Schedule the meeting during the last week of the person's employment.

3. During the interview you should:
- Meet in a neutral place. Your office may be intimidating. Consider having an exit luncheon for someone who has been a valued employee.
- Arrange the physical layout to promote a problem-solving discussion rather than a boss-subordinate interview. Sit next to the person rather than on the opposite side of a desk.

- Prepare to listen without being defensive. Bring a notebook to record details.
- Get as much information as possible by covering
  - your perception of your own leadership and interaction with others in the department;
  - details about the job held, especially any difficulties you were not aware of; what the person enjoyed about the job;
  - any corporate policies and procedures that prevented the person from doing the job effectively or caused annoyance;
  - anything else the person feels you should know.
- If the associate is vague, prod with specific, open-ended questions. For example, you could ask questions such as:
  - Could you give me an example of that?
  - Could you be more specific?
  - Tell me more about that!
- Find out about the associate's new job. This information could give you ideas about what is wrong now. You might ask
  - what attracted the individual to the job;
  - what aspects of the job were appealing;
  - how the new work environment will differ;
  - how salary and benefits compare.

4. After the interview you should:
- Collate your information. Pass on important data to those who can take corrective action. Reflect on and then fix those things over which you have control.
- If the information gathered has been contentious, consider conducting a follow-up interview by phone or in person. Better still, consider having someone other than you do the interview, if you feel that this will enhance the objectivity of information-gathering. You may find that the person's perspective has changed once she is outside the organization.

Feedback

Giving

We prefer to be praised rather than punished,
and prefer to be punished rather than ignored.

DR. JOYCE BROWN

Do no reprove him in such a way that you
bring sin upon yourself, such as by shaming him
through reproving him in public.

A. S. HARTOM

The most challenging and important communication skill is the ability to let people know when you are unhappy with something they have done. Letting them know about your discontent in a way that focuses on the problem, not the person, will lead to trust, understanding, and mutual respect. This important skill can be used at work, but it is important to do this in your home life too. Here's the secret to doing it well:

1. Do it soon. Don't let the problem fester. Your relationship with your associates will be poisoned if they have done something to upset you and you do not deal with the issue.

2. Do it in private. Allowing other people to see and hear the discussion will exacerbate the problem and involve more people than are needed.

3. Get an invitation. Ask the person when it is convenient to meet. This will get buy-in to the process. In the unlikely event that the employee refuses, you will need to be more assertive. Agree to a venue. The feedback should be obtained as soon after the problem occurs as possible.

4. Be specific. Tell the employee exactly what you know without diluting your thoughts into generalities. If possible, give numbers, dates, and places. Avoid using the words such as "always" or "never." It is not necessary to exaggerate in order to make your point.

5. Be assertive. Work hard to satisfy your own needs. Being assertive means:
- Using the "I" word, never the "you" word. Saying "I have a problem and need your help" will garner greater support than "You are doing this or that."
- Speaking with a firm, deliberate voice.
- Maintaining eye contact.
- Projecting confidence in your posture.

6. Choose your words carefully. Don't use inflammatory language or the person will focus on the way feedback is being given rather than on the message.

7. Involve the person in finding a satisfactory solution. Ask how he can help. Don't tell him how to solve the problem, as this will reduce the buy-in necessary to have the issue resolved.

8. Check and clarify key discussion points so there will be no mis-understanding.

9. Summarize your understanding with agreements. You could say, "So what I'm hearing you say is ———. Is that correct?"

10. Summarize the discussion at the end so that you both clearly understand what was said and what was agreed upon.

11. Acknowledge the person afterwards when her behaviour is in accordance with your agreement.

Feedback

*G*etting feedback is probably the greatest opportunity for you to grow, learn, and improve your relationships with others. Why? Because you are constantly being given feedback. It happens daily. To ignore it is to lose the opportunity to adjust your behaviour and attitudes. Here is how to take full advantage of messages others are giving you:

1. Be receptive to feedback. If you're not sure how you're doing, ask people you trust to evaluate you.

2. Listen, listen, listen. Let the person giving feedback finish before you interrupt. Listen to be influenced. If the information is extensive, consider making notes.

3. When the feedback is done, summarize and echo back to the "giver" your understanding of what he has said.

4. Thank the person for the feedback. Let her know how useful it was. More important, tell her how you're going to use the information to change and improve.

5. Try not to explain the reason for doing less than expected. Take time to think, so your emotions can be put aside.

6. Ask the person who gave you the feedback to give you feedback later on, particularly if he sees a change.

Goal-Setting
Personal

If a man hasn't found something he
will die for, he isn't to live.

MARTIN LUTHER KING, JR.

*Y*ou will enhance your career and effectiveness by focusing on yearly, monthly, weekly, and even daily goals. Your goals are your road map to a successful future. They will determine the direction in which you are headed and ensure that you reach your destination. Here's how to set goals:

1. Identify goals that are consistent with your values, beliefs, and life philosophies.

2. Commit your goals to paper. Don't rely on your memory. Put them in a place where you will see them often.

3. Determine your goals. Make sure they are SMART, that is:
   - **S**pecific ("I want to retire with $2 million in the bank by age sixty-five" is preferable to saying "I want to make tons of money in order to retire");

- **M**easurable;
- **A**greed upon;
- **R**ealistic;
- **T**ime-based.

4. Ensure that your goals are in sync with your morals and values. If you're like most people, millions of dollars won't make you happy if you have had to exploit people in the process of making the money.

5. Prioritize your goals. Focus on those that have greater meaning to you in terms of your personal beliefs. If community volunteer work is something you place a great value on, for example, find ways of avoiding overtime and give yourself time to do the community work that appeals to you more.

6. Break your goals into short-, medium-, and long-range plans. This will allow you to stay focused and in touch with your final goal.

7. Make people aware of your goals. Tell a friend, mentor, and even your worst enemy. Contract with someone who will meet with you regularly to ensure that you remain on track.

8. Ask yourself if the goal has true value for you. It could just be an excuse to avoid doing something important but unpleasant.

9. Visualize yourself achieving your goal. Your vision will give you a sense of excitement and encourage you to keep on trying. At the same time, your work goals, although important, should not become an obsession. If this happens, you will upset the equilibrium between personal life and work, resulting in physical and mental deterioration.

10. Act on your goals regularly. True success comes from taking small steps. It is unlikely that you will make immediate huge gains without an enormous amount of luck. Therefore, focus on short-term goals that will lead to the longer goal. Try to do something each day that will move you closer to your goal.

11. Review your goals regularly. For example, monthly goals should be reviewed daily to keep you focused.

12. Celebrate your achievements, no matter how small they may be.

Harassment

*The first step in the evolution of ethics is a sense
of solidarity with other human beings.*

ALBERT SCHWEITZER

*H*arassment refers to comments and conduct that is known, or ought reasonably to be known, to be unwelcome.

1. Did you know that:

- Harassment covers a broad ranges of issues? These include:
  - ancestry;
  - place of origin;
  - record of offences;
  - marital status;
  - ethnic origin;
  - age;
  - colour;
  - citizenship;
  - handicap;
  - sexual orientation.
  - race;
  - creed;
  - sex;
  - family status;
- Management can be held liable for the actions of its employees?
- People in positions of authority, including union representatives, can be held legally accountable if they have not responded effectively?
- Men and women see the problem of harassment differently?

2. Ensure that there are no reprisals against the complainant.

3. Common myths about harassment are that
   - the problem does not exist if no one has complained;
   - educating employees means that they are likely to use the information against the employer;
   - the problem will go away or fix itself if it is not attended to.

4. As an employee, you should
   - familiarize yourself with your corporation's policy on harassment and provide copies of the policy to your associates;
   - campaign for a policy to be established if none exists;
   - let people know that harassment will not be tolerated.

5. Increase awareness of the problem by having your people watch educational videos during working hours, or by circulating relevant literature.

6. Become a role model of non-sexist, non-racist behaviour by treating people with respect. Use language that is gender and race neutral.

7. If you become aware of harassment in your work area and are in a position of authority:
   - Deal with the issue right away. Failure to do so may give the impression that you condone the act.
   - Collect the facts. Do so assertively.

8. Find out
   - what happened;
   - who the alleged harasser is;
   - if the alleged harasser knew that his or her conduct was unwelcome;
   - when and where the behaviour occurred;
   - if there were any witnesses;

- if the harassed person has told anyone else;
- how often and for how long this behaviour has been going on;
- what evidence exists related to this allegation.

9. Confine your investigation to those involved or witnesses. Do not pour fuel on the fire by discussing the issue with people who are not involved or those who do not need to know.

10. If there are allegations of sexual harassment, determine whether
- the advances interfere with the complainant's work performance;
- the harassment has created a hostile or offensive environment;
- the complainant has been explicitly or implicitly threatened with job loss if sexual favours are withheld;
- the accused has based a decision to hire on receiving sexual favours.

11. If the offence is minor, warn the person immediately in writing.

12. For serious offences, such as offering promotions in return for sexual favours, the accused will probably have to be dismissed.

13. Maintain the complainant's confidentiality whenever possible.

14. If you are harassed:
- Make your feelings known immediately to the harasser.
- If you feel that the transgression was minor, and that it may not occur again, you could choose to leave it.
- If the matter is important to you, make someone in authority aware of the situation immediately.
- Always be assertive. You have every right to demand respect from your fellow employees.

Health and Wellness

Taking Care of Your Physical Well-Being

Blessed are those who hunger and thirst,
for they are sticking to their diets.

UNKNOWN

If we are to function as happy, productive individuals we must take very seriously the well-known saying "You are what you eat." In 1988 the U.S. surgeon general's *Report on Nutrition and Health* claimed that more than two-thirds of deaths in North America are nutrition-related. Bad nutrition causes degenerative diseases such as cancer, cardiovascular disease (heart disease, stroke, and atherosclerosis), diabetes, and more. The good news is that these diseases are generally preventable if we take seriously what goes into our bodies.

1. Improve your physical well-being by exercising. Physical exercise will reduce your risk of heart disease, diabetes, obesity, osteoporosis, colon cancer, hypertension, and stroke. Regular exercise helps reduce stress and anxiety, improves sleep, and reduces mental fatigue. It also contributes to improved self-esteem, psychological well-being, and a healthy body weight. General guidelines for fitness are as follows:

- Exercise three to five times a week for twenty to sixty minutes at a time.
- Variety is best for the body and good for the mind. So walk one day, hike another, and go dancing the next!
- Include some weight-bearing exercises in your program. This builds bone mass and prevents deteriorating muscles associated with ageing.
- For effective weight loss, exercise at lower intensity for longer periods of time.
- Stretch the entire body before and after exercising. Stretching before will prevent muscle pulls; stretching after will prevent stiffness. Hold each position for at least thirty seconds.

2. Follow these guidelines for an improved diet:
- Change your drinking habits. Reduce your intake of artificial liquids such as coffee, tea, and pop. Increase your consumption of water. Drink up to eight glasses a day. Water improves our digestion, cools us down, circulates nutrients around the body, and promotes the excretion of wastes from the body. It also dilutes and flushes out toxins from our systems.
- Choose water that has been filtered. Acquire a filtering system from a reputable professional who has no allegiance to any one system. City water may contain as many as 500 different disease-causing bacteria, viruses, and parasites. Our drinking water is often drawn from polluted sources and is purified by chlorination, fluoridation, and sometimes ammonia.
- Relax while you are eating. Reading or watching TV is not necessarily relaxing, as these diversions do not allow the parasympathetic system to operate optimally and digest our food. When we eat on the run, we are using the sympathetic system, which merely deposits undigested food into the stomach before it gets passed out.

- Chew your food extensively — experts say about thirty-five times. This promotes better digestion because our saliva has enzymes that initiate breakdown while the food is still in the mouth.
- Eat more whole-grain products. Regular white flour, white pasta, and white rice add less to our diet than do their brown counterparts. Look for ancient grains such as kamut, spelt, and quinoa in your supermarket.
- Eat more fresh fruit and vegetables — five to ten servings per day are recommended. Choose vegetables that have a rich green, red, or yellow colour, as they contain antioxidants that help prevent degenerative diseases such as cancer.
- Buy less shiny or waxy fruits and vegetables, as these coatings may trap pesticides and other toxins.
- Wash fruit and vegetables with vinegar, lemon juice, and water to remove surface pesticides.
- Eat two to four servings of calcium-containing products such as broccoli. If you can't get sufficient amounts, consider a supplement such as calcium citrate (never carbonate), with magnesium and vitamin D.
- Eat two to three servings of protein products daily. Switch from red meat to soy products (tofu), beans, seeds, and eggs.
- Eat more fish, especially salmon, sardines, and other deep-sea fish that contain the "good" fats.
- Choose leaner cuts and skin-free poultry if your eating habits demand meat.
- Don't avoid all fats and oils. Olive oil is best. Other nutritious oils include flax, hemp, and evening primrose. These make great salad dressings and popcorn toppings. Commercially prepared oils contain virtually no nutrients.
- Reduce your intake of saturated fats commonly found in butter. Hydrogenated oils such as margarine are not recommended either.

- Avoid heating oils, as they produce free radicals that can cause degenerative diseases over time. "Stable" saturated oils such as butter and coconut oil are preferable, particularly if used in moderation.

3. Other eating tips are:
   - Use frozen vegetables over canned vegetables, but fresh is best.
   - Read labels. Avoid processed foods that have many ingredients that preserve shelf-life.
   - Don't be fooled by no-fat labels, since unused sugars (carbohydrates) are converted into fats.

Health and Wellness

Taking Care of Your Mental Health

*Love cures people – both the ones who
give it and the ones who receive it.*

DR. KARL MENNINGER

*W*ellness is about taking care of yourself. It is an empowered process that recognizes the connection between your mental and physical well-being. Wellness is not a fad. It can require many changes for most of us, but its implementation is a journey requiring one change at a time. As we improve our living habits, we begin to make good habits a way of life rather than a short-term change.

1. Maintain a great attitude. Your outlook will improve if you:
- Think positive. See the glass as half full, not half empty. See the good in people rather than the bad.
- Be optimistic. Expect good things to happen and, more often than not, they will.
- Lighten up. Have fun. Enjoy even stupid movies. Behave like a child. Learn to play pranks (without hurting or offending people) that will promote laughter.
- Subscribe to an Internet joke site that will send you a smile each day. Pass on the good ones.

- Make yourself the top priority. There is value in being a people-pleaser, but only if those people come second. Your needs are paramount. You'll never really be helpful to others unless you feel happy about your own life.
- Avoid being a control freak. Cut down on the number of decisions you want to make for others. If you have kids, learn to give them more scope as they mature and show increasing responsibility. Learn to ask permission if you have suggestions for others, instead of telling them what to do.
- Know what gives you pleasure and do it often! Spoil yourself. Indulge. For example, if you have favourite recording artists, buy their latest CDs and play them at every opportunity.
- Share your spirit, time, and wealth. Learn to give of yourself. Your psychic income will far exceed what you give away.

2. Enhance your relationships with others.
- Never take for granted the relationships with people you care about. Work at them constantly to improve them.
- Validate your relationships. Let people know how much you appreciate them. And let them know when they've done something that offends you.
- Find a confidant who enjoys listening to you when you need a friend. Avoid "confidants" who want to solve your problems or give you uncalled-for advice. Reciprocate when needed. Listen to people who need to vent without interruption. Don't evaluate their concerns; simply understand their feelings.
- Do things that give you pleasure. Have a chocolate at the end of the day. Have a low-fat pudding occasionally.
- Spend more time with friends, particularly those to whom you can bare your soul. Focus on people who like to touch and hug — they will provide you with the emotional support often lacking in the superficiality of modern urban living.

Hiring

Conducting the Interview

$\mathcal{A}$s an empowered team member, you can expect to be involved in decisions about who to hire into the department. After all, who is better able to judge the technical skills of potential candidates than the people who do the job! But remember, it is important to find people who will fit in with other team members, so morale can remain high. So take this challenge seriously, as a bad orange can poison the whole bag! Here are some interviewing tips for you:

1. When the candidate enters the room, greet her with a firm hand-shake. Smile to relax her. Indicate your enthusiasm at having the opportunity to meet her and find out more about her.

2. Avoid generic questions — they tend to produce generic responses. Find out instead about specific situations involving the interviewee. Don't, for example, ask, "How would you discipline an employee?" Phrase your question as, "Tell me about an instance where you had to reprimand someone." Follow up with questions to draw out the interviewee. Find out why he reprimanded the person, what happened afterwards, and what he might have learned from the incident.

_3._ Using the application form as a guide, question the interviewee about
  - gaps in employment history;
  - particular accomplishments;
  - references you can contact.

_4._ Get to the facts of the matter, especially when the applicant has presented a professionally prepared resumé. Question the interviewee closely about achievements or qualifications that seem overinflated.

_5._ Keep your questions in logical order so you can get an in-depth perspective on important issues. If you skip from subject to subject, you will confuse the interviewee and generate irrelevant discussion.

_6._ Don't lead the candidate by giving the answer along with the question. For example, you would not want to phrase a question as "Do you think it's wrong to reprimand someone in the presence of his colleagues?"

_7._ Allow for silences. The interviewee will need time to think about questions, and to elaborate on statements already made. Encourage further comments with leading remarks. For example, if the candidate says, "I had one or two problems with my last boss," you might respond, "Problems?" in a neutral tone to elicit further information.

_8._ Describe some challenges the candidate may encounter in the job and ask for ideas on how to deal with them. Find out if she has had to deal with similar situations.

_9._ Make sure that critical issues are fully dealt with. Use "what" and "how" questions to steer the candidate back on course if he wanders. Avoid "why" questions, as they can lead to defensive reactions.

10. If the interviewee falls back on generalizations or jargon, ask her for specific definitions of terms.

11. Remember that human-rights legislation prevents you from asking about a person's
- race;
- religion;
- age;
- marital status;
- country of birth;
- family plans;
- criminal history;
- financial position;
- sexual orientation.

12. Watch out for the following warning signs:
- inappropriate dress;
- signs of anxiety beyond normal nervousness, such as excessive fidgeting;
- unwillingness to make eye contact (but be aware of cultural differences);
- lack of satisfactory reason for employment gaps on resumé;
- inappropriate remarks about previous employers or colleagues.

13. After you have all the information you need about the candidate, discuss the job in question, describing tasks involved and criteria for success. Let the candidate consider whether the job is a good fit.

14. Describe your organization and its culture, and explain your expectations about the job. Leave time for the candidate to ask questions — these questions, or the lack of them, will reveal much about his character and interest in the position.

15. At the close of the interview:
- Explain the next steps to the candidate, including whether there will be second interviews and when decisions will be made.
- Be honest with the candidate. If you know immediately that there isn't a good fit, tell her, tactfully explaining why. Don't leave her with unrealistic hopes, but be careful not to damage her self-esteem. Let her know what further skills or experience she needs to acquire, and whether you will be keeping her resumé on file.

16. After the interview, use a standardized form to evaluate the candidates consistently. The following categories should be considered:
- experience;
- education;
- skills and interests;
- dress and grooming;
- personality;
- voice;
- suitability to the job.

Not all of these categories are of equal importance, so design a weighting system to emphasize categories that are of greatest importance to you and to the job.

17. Once you have a short list, do a reference check. Appropriate referees include former employers, colleagues, subordinates, and customers.

18. Ask for proof of professional qualifications. If transcripts are not available, check claims of degrees, diplomas, or certificates with the relevant institutions or associations.

USEFUL INTERVIEW QUESTIONS

- If you got the job, what would you do in the first month?
- What would you do if faced with a 10 percent budget cut?
- What is your least favourite aspect of your present job? Why?
- What is the thing you like most about your present job? Why?
- Describe the best boss you ever had and what you liked about him.
- Describe the worst boss you ever had. Why was she the worst?
- How do you and your boss think alike? How do you differ?
- Describe the most difficult thing in your present job and explain why it is difficult.
- What are your long-term career goals? How will you reach them?
- What was your most important achievement in your last job? How did you do it?
- How do you respond to criticism?
- Describe an instance where you disciplined an employee. What happened afterwards?
- What was your worst moment in a job? How did you deal with it?
- What is your one major weakness? How are you trying to improve?
- How might your last boss describe you, in five words?
- How would you like me to remember you in relation to this job?

Hiring

$\mathcal{T}$he uniqueness of each candidate and interview will help determine how to approach reference checks. However, you may want to:

1. Confirm items on the candidate's resumé, such as past employment dates and positions; accuracy of claims about achievements; competence; superior/subordinate relationships; circumstances of leaving past jobs.

2. Use open-ended questions about the candidate's strengths; weaknesses; contributions to the organization; most valued qualities; decision to leave, and its impact on the organization; relationship to bosses, peers, and subordinates.

3. Encourage elaboration of explanations with questions such as "Can you explain that?" or "Can you tell me more?"

4. Follow up on any hunches about the candidate that you may have developed during the interview.

5. Ask the referee if there is anything significant you have missed asking about.

Influencing People

You make more friends by becoming interested in other people than by trying to interest other people in yourself.

DALE CARNEGIE

$\mathcal{E}$ach of us is dependent on others in our organization. Influencing people to gain commitment for new ideas is crucial. Here are some ideas to improve your effectiveness:

1. Acknowledge that you are dependent on others. Develop a collaborative attitude.

2. Treat people with respect, consideration, and dignity. They will do the same with you.

3. Deal with differences with your peers directly. Avoid appealing to those above you to exert authority over your peers. You need to be able to influence them by yourself.

4. Help people out whenever possible. Do them favours. You will then be able to legitimately ask them to return favours when you need them.

5. Wait for important opportunities to collect IOUs from people, especially if they have
- unique skills;
- specialized knowledge;
- "exotic" information.

Your dependency on them becomes balanced by their dependency on you.

6. Treat people as equals. Don't abuse the power that comes from a higher position in the organization. People will retaliate later. Also, pulling rank will prevent the development of the trust and respect needed for genuine co-operation.

7. Keep communications upbeat and positive. Focus on the good rather than the bad.

8. Treat individuals as special and unique. Focus on the things that motivate them.

9. Find out what people's hot buttons are. Let them know how you can help them get what they want. Paint a picture of your needs that is compatible with theirs.

10. Use your power to influence them.
- The power of legitimacy is established when you present information that looks good by finding substantial evidence from credible sources that backs up your point of view.
- The power of precedent is used when you can demonstrate that your idea has worked before in similar circumstances. A successful pilot program is an excellent precedent.
- The power of competition comes into play if you can show how your idea can improve the organization before others do. Also,

if you show that you have others interested in your idea, you will motivate more interest than if you don't.

- The power of rationality suggests that facts and data will be more persuasive than opinions.
- The power of knowledge works for you when you can demonstrate that you are the expert in the field.
- The power of numbers suggests that if there are many people who feel the same way as you, and you can prove it, your chances of influencing others will be improved considerably.
- The power of rank indicates that you have support from people high up in the organization.

Influencing
Senior Management

Strong beliefs win strong men, and then make them stronger.

WALTER BAGEHOT

_H_aving great ideas can prove frustrating, especially if you don't have the ability to sell them to someone who has the power to approve implementation. Here's how to persuade those above you to accept your ideas:

1. Prepare thoroughly before you meet. The more important and controversial the idea, the more you need to be prepared.

2. Be frank with yourself. Do you really care about the issue? Can you project enthusiasm? If not, be realistic about the outcome.

3. Get as many backup facts as you can. Your opinion is more important to you than it is to others. The more data you have, the more rational you can be and the greater will be your influence.

4. Anticipate senior management's reaction to your proposal. Prepare effective responses to any resistance. Rehearse your presentation with an associate, if possible. Have written documentation to support key aspects of your proposal.

5. Collect ideas from those to whom you will be selling your idea. Incorporate these ideas into your pitch. This will earn you some measure of buy-in before you start.

6. Greet people warmly. A firm handshake that lingers a second longer than usual gives the impression that you like the other person.

7. Present your ideas concisely. You will not have ages to convince people. Managers' time is valuable and their attention spans are short. If you can't convince them in five to seven minutes, you probably will never convince them. If their interest grows and they have more questions, the discussion will go beyond your anticipated time.

8. Speak the language of the people with whom you are dealing. Find out what the issues of the day are. For example, if cost-saving is important, show how your idea will save money. If quality is the issue, show how your idea can reduce errors or customer returns.

9. Never make exaggerated claims that can be proven false or promises you cannot fulfil.

10. Give compliments whenever they are due. Genuine compliments disarm people and spark their interest in having further discussions with you.

11. Look optimistic and upbeat. Smile often. People are more receptive to ideas presented in friendly conversation those presented than in doom-and-gloom interchanges.

12. Show interest in their reactions. This will indicate your determination to satisfy them.

13. If you are unable to get approval at your first meeting, ask for a follow-up session. Find out what obstacles remain before you can get the go-ahead. Collect any additional information that may be required to fully satisfy your managers.

14. Thank people for their time in a memo. Confirm the issues that need to be dealt with prior to approval.

15. Don't let outstanding issues drag on. Show your enthusiasm by dealing with such issues quickly.

Leadership

Leaders are like eagles. They don't flock –
you find them one at a time.

SUCCESSORIES INC.

Leadership and learning are indispensable to each other.

JOHN F. KENNEDY

*L*eadership is about influence. If you can influence people, you are exerting leadership. Hence, anyone can lead in an organization — you do not have to have a title to do so. In fact, as organizations continue to redefine the way they operate, people are being asked to take more responsibility and initiative — all key leadership attributes. As you prepare for a leadership role in your organization, measure yourself against these attributes:

1. Leaders have a clear vision of where they are going. And they don't keep their vision a secret — they share it with those around them in the hope of mobilizing them to move in the same direction.

2. Leaders are consistent. They are true to their principles and values at all times.

3. Leaders do what they expect of others. They "walk the talk."

4. Leaders are not threatened by competence. Outstanding peers energize them. And they are quick to give credit to those who have earned it.

5. Leaders enjoy seeing others around them increase their skills and confidence. They share their knowledge to enable colleagues to take on more challenging tasks and responsibilities.

6. Leaders don't betray trust. They can treat confidential information professionally.

7. Leaders are concerned about getting things done. They don't get embroiled in political infighting, gossip, and back-stabbing. They encourage those around them to do likewise.

8. Leaders confront issues as they arise. They don't procrastinate. If something needs fixing, they do it right away, even if it's uncomfortable. The longer things are left, the more difficult they become.

9. Leaders recognize superior performance. They are generous with praise to the person concerned and to others who should know.

10. Leaders are flexible. They welcome change. They don't stick to an old position simply because it is more comfortable.

11. Leaders are adaptable. They see change as an opportunity rather than a threat.

12. Leaders are human. They make mistakes. When they do so, they readily admit it.

13. Leaders learn from their mistakes. They use errors as a way to improve their skills.

14. Leaders enjoy being challenged. They are prepared to take risks and encourage others to do the same. If they fail, they treat the exercise as a learning experience.

15. Leaders focus on the future, not the past. They anticipate trends and prepare for them.

16. Leaders are open to new ideas. They demonstrate their receptiveness by supporting change.

17. Leaders treat staff members as individuals. They give closer attention to those who need it, and lots of space to those who deserve it.

18. Leaders encourage and reward co-operation within and between teams.

19. Leaders develop guidelines for the team. They enlarge the guidelines as the team becomes willing to accept more responsibility.

20. Leaders change their role according to the demands of the team. For example, they function more as coaches or facilitators when needed.

21. Leaders listen to fellow team members. They don't interrupt others, and they allow themselves to be influenced.

22. Leaders involve people in finding new ways to achieve goals.

23. Leaders create the opportunity for group participation, recognizing that only team members can make the choice to participate.

Learning

Becoming a Better Reader

The illiterate of the future will not be the person who cannot read. It will be the person who does not know how to learn.

ALVIN TOFFLER

$\mathcal{W}$e are confronted by increased volumes of information through e-mails, regular mail, junk mail, books, magazines, etc. Having an ability to sort through information quickly and grasp the essence of the message is a real asset. Here's how you can reduce your reading time and improve your comprehension:

1. Improve your concentration and focus in one of two ways:

- Use your hand as a guide to your reading. Put your hand on the page just below what you are reading so you cannot skip to anything below.

- Use a blank sheet of paper or index card to block the information above the line you are reading. This will prevent you from backtracking and force you to concentrate harder as you read.

2. Test your understanding of each page by jotting down key ideas. This will force you to think as you are reading and to formulate a model of key ideas in your mind. This process can be done by

- noting key ideas in written form;
- drawing a picture that describes the key concept.

3. For lengthy articles or academic information, resort to skimming. This technique enables you to group key ideas without getting sidetracked by "filler" details. Follow the train of thought of the author by

- reading the introduction;
- reading the conclusion;
- picking key sentences that contain the main message — usually the last sentence of each paragraph;
- highlighting key ideas with a highlighter marker.

When you are done, check your understanding by noting key ideas or drawing a picture of what you have learned.

Learning

Becoming a Life-Long Learner

Empty pockets never held a man back.
Only empty heads and empty hearts can do that.

NORMAN VINCENT PEALE

$\mathcal{L}$earning is a process, not an event. Becoming a life-long learner requires that we do things daily to acquire knowledge and learn new skills. Learning for the sake of learning is less valuable than learning to improve our moral character and become a more effective employee, life partner, and parent. Here are some ideas to help you achieve this.

1. Create the mindset that learning is important. Open your mind and your heart to new experiences. Recognize that
- you can learn all your life;
- learning is a natural life process;
- learning can sometimes be difficult, especially as it may challenge your beliefs.

2. Look at the big picture. Learning, life, and all that you do are connected.

3. Learning is spiritual. Be open to the impact of spirituality.

4. Men and women learn differently. Give yourself the freedom to learn in a way most comfortable to you.

5. Don't prejudge how a particular type of learning will fit into your life. Be open to new horizons.

6. Find out your learning style preference. "Test" for your preference. Are you prone to want to contemplate before trying a new situation? Or do you prefer to have a go and learn as you are doing things? The first group — thinkers — learn best by
- getting lots of information up front;
- having ample preparation time;
- listening and watching;
- working with more structure;
- seeing models of each concept;
- having a plan to follow.

The doers, on the other hand, learn best by
- having lots of variety;
- keeping active;
- getting hands-on practice;
- having to perform spontaneously;
- having information that is relevant to their situations.

7. Be curious. Learn to ask lots of questions, just as a child does, but avoid doing it to the point of being annoying.

8. Learn from mistakes. We all make them. Figure out what you did wrong and avoid doing it again.

9. If you're not sure what you did wrong, ask others. Listen. Don't be defensive. Make notes to show you care about their ideas. Thank them for the advice and time, whether you agree with them or not.

10. If you've made a mistake on something you do infrequently, note the solution in a file that is easily accessible. When you need to do that task again, you can avoid making the same mistake.

11. Take the initiative to find out how you are doing. Don't wait for your annual performance review. If you're doing things differently, ask your boss for feedback. That's how you'll know if your new ideas are appreciated.

12. Use spare time to learn. Any time you're in a line-up or on public transit, consider reading an article of interest. Also, access books on tape that you can listen to in your car or on a Walkman.

13. Subscribe to newsletters that provide you with interesting information succinctly. The Internet has many free services that are downloaded daily. Scan these pages quickly and zero in on things that are helpful. Try to use them as soon as possible in order to gain immediate benefit.

14. Seek out opportunities to learn.
- Find people who have travelled, come from other countries, worked in interesting jobs, or been to some unusual workshops. Find out as much as you can about their experiences.
- Volunteer for any pilot training programs that take place in your organization. Offer to attend outside workshops with the understanding that you will report back on what you learned so the value can be multiplied.
- Take a look at the workbooks of others who have been to seminars and workshops. Buy them lunch or coffee so you can pepper them with questions after you have skimmed through their notes.

15. Subscribe to magazines that will give you the technical knowledge to enhance your career. Or subscribe each year to a magazine in a totally unrelated field, but one you might benefit from spiritually.

16. Seek out smart (not arrogant) people. Spend time with them. Ask them lots of questions. Find out their sources for good ideas.

17. Watch fewer soaps and sitcoms on TV. Become selective. Look for programs that add some intellectual capital for you.

18. Find a mentor. Seek out someone who has a wealth of lifetime experiences to share. Set up a monthly meeting at which you can bounce ideas off the mentor or draw on his life experience.

19. Realize that every day presents a new learning opportunity. Some less obvious opportunities include:
- benchmarking the activities of the best in the business;
- covering for others who are on holiday;
- crises;
- delegated tasks;
- demonstrations;
- meetings;
- helping someone else to learn;
- job rotation;
- networking;
- performance appraisals;
- special projects;
- videos;
- working with consultants.

Learning

Taking Responsibility for Improving
Your Skills Through Training

*Only the curious will learn and only the resolute overcome
the obstacles of learning. The quest quotient has always
exceeded me more than the intelligence quotient.*

EUGENE S. WILSON

*I*ncreasingly, organizations are looking to their staff members to take
responsibility for their own learning and careers. Many organizations are
cutting back on sending people to outside workshops, seeing these as
more of a perk than an opportunity to build skills. Research shows that
people learn very little by sitting in a classroom — and use even less.
The most powerful ways of learning are by experiencing the skills and
teaching others. These should be key parts of your learning plan. Here
are some principles to bear in mind as you create your development plan
with your boss. The key criteria for a learning plan are that it be:

1. *Related to the business plan.* Focus on skills that are in keeping
with expanding the business or improving customer service.

2. *Specific.* You can't learn generalities. Your plan should detail the
specific skills from which you could benefit. Communication is too
general. Listening or conflict resolution is more specific. The

plan must also be specific in terms of dates and courses you will take.

3. *Appropriate.* You should avail yourself of the opportunity to learn according to your own style. There are many theories on learning styles, but most focus on the degree of self-direction you require. Some people prefer a high degree of autonomy and can learn on their own. Others need more directions and benefit from more conventional coaching. Self-directed learning opportunities include computer-based training, self-help books, personal research, courses on the Internet, and mentoring. Conventional learning usually takes the form of in-house workshops or outside programs.

4. *Suited to personality.* Your personality also plays a role in determining your learning style. Extroverted people like to be active and will do things with enthusiasm. They will quickly try things out without thinking too deeply about them first. On the other hand, introverts need to think before acting. They need to conceptualize issues first, clearly thinking through the options and consequences before getting involved. Courses that are self-paced might suit them better than a fast-paced interactive workshop.

5. *Useful.* You should be able to apply the skills right away. There is no point in learning something for possible use six months down the road. Most people — as busy as they are — need to use the skills within two weeks of the course or they will forget them.

6. *Realistic.* The plan should not overburden you so that you are learning something new before you've had a chance to perfect the previous skill.

Listening

There was an old owl that lived in an oak,
The more he heard, the less he spoke;
The less he spoke, the more he heard,
O, if men were all like that wise bird!

PUNCH MAGAZINE, LXVIII, 155 [1875]

*W*hy do people have two ears and one mouth? It's probably because we are meant to listen twice as much as we talk. Or is it because listening is so much more difficult than talking? Listening shows that you care, that you have empathy and are prepared to be influenced. It also allows you to understand where the person you are communicating with is coming from. Here are the golden rules of listening:

1. Give the other person your undivided attention. Don't do other work or take calls while you are listening.

2. Talk less or don't talk at all. This will force the other person to speak.

3. Find a quiet place to listen. Avoid places that are noisy or have other distractions.

4. Listen to be influenced. Concentrate. Don't allow your mind to be absorbed with developing rebuttals.

5. Let people finish their points. Only when they keep repeating the same point should you interrupt and indicate your understanding.

6. Show that you are interested. Do this by nodding or periodically saying yes and leaning forward.

7. Maintain eye contact without staring.

8. Show positive body language. Lean forward. Look interested. Face the person who is talking to you. Smile occasionally.

9. Ask for clarification if you are not sure you have clearly understood a message. Or summarize your understanding by saying, "So what I hear you saying is —. Is that right?"

10. Ask open-ended questions. Such questions help get at what people feel rather than eliciting responses you want to hear.

11. Be empathetic. Even if you disagree with another's views and sentiments, you are learning; try to see things from her perspective.

12. Be patient. Some people take a little more time to articulate their thoughts. Wait until they have completed their points of view before responding.

13. Watch for non-verbal reactions during the conversation. Most of what people think doesn't come out of their mouths. Observe their facial expressions, posture, gestures, and eye movements to evaluate what they are *thinking*.

14. Keep pace with the speaker. Don't jump to conclusions or fill in the gaps.

15. Allow people to finish their own sentences. Don't assume you know what they're going to say..

16. Let others finish before you confirm your understanding. Train yourself to count slowly to five before interjecting or responding.

17. Learn to let short, comfortable silences descend on a conversation. Silence encourages the other person to fill the void.

Measuring
Your Performance

$\mathcal{T}$hink about your favourite sports team. Have you ever noticed how well the players perform compared with people in your organization? Why is this so? One reason is that people on a sports team always know how they are doing. Their performance is measured so they can see and feel the effects of their efforts. And they can celebrate achievements or identify opportunities for improvement.

One of the most effective ways to measure team performance is performance indexing. The system is based on the balanced scorecard concept, in that it can

— measure a number of indicators on one scorecard;

— reflect the interests of the customers, shareholders, and staff simultaneously;

— measure the past (financial results), as well as the future (innovation).

Performance indexing is a powerful tool for motivating a team or its individual members. You can use it to

— plan improvements;

— set goals;

— review achievements;

— celebrate improvements.

Take these steps to set up your own scorecard:

Step 1.

Define why you come to work. Create your own mission.

Before creating your scorecard, you need to define your purpose. This purpose, or mission, should be based on the mission of your organization. For example, if your corporate mission is to provide exceptional service and be the supplier of choice, then your mission should reflect similar lofty ideals. A simple formula for writing up a mission is to answer these six questions:

- Who are you? Write your name and job title (1).
- What do you do? Describe what you do (2).
- How do you carry out this activity? Describe key dimensions, such as timeliness, quality, or cost-effectiveness (3).
- Who do you serve? Describe your customers, specifying their market segments, if necessary (4).
- Where are your customers? Describe your geographic coverage (5).
- Why do you do this job? State benefits for yourself, the customer, and the organization or department (6).

Once these questions have been answered, put them into the framework below.

Who _____ What _____
             (1)   (2)

How _____ Who _____
             (3)   (4)

Where _____ Why _____
             (5)   (6)

Create a sentence or two from the above elements to serve as your mission statement.

Step 2.

Identify key performance indicators that will track whether you are operating according to your mission.

Identify the most important categories of performance. These categories typically relate to

- quality (satisfying the customer the first time);
- timeliness (responsiveness of service);
- cost-effectiveness (profitability);
- health and safety;
- your satisfaction.

Where possible, pick performance indicators that are

- easy to collect;
- readily available;
- accurate;
- within your control/influence.

Step 3.

Determine existing performance levels.

Average your performance over the previous three months or another period. As you gather data, you will see how suitable your indicator is. If, for example, it becomes extremely costly to collect information, the indicator's value should be questioned.

Current performance levels should be entered into the matrix that appears on the next page. Enter information in the boxes corresponding to the score of 3 to provide more room for improvement than for decline on the 0–10 scale.

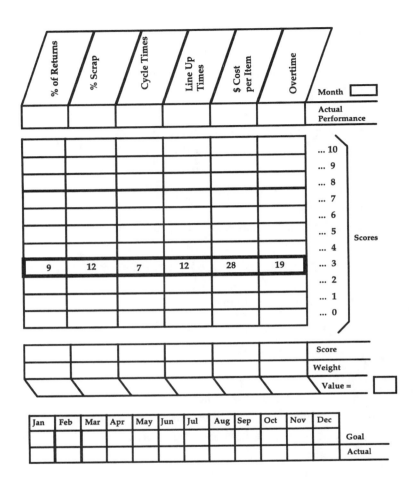

						Month ▭
% of Returns	% Scrap	Cycle Times	Line Up Times	$ Cost per Item	Overtime	Actual Performance

						... 10
						... 9
						... 8
						... 7
						... 6
						... 5
						... 4
9	**12**	**7**	**12**	**28**	**19**	... 3
						... 2
						... 1
						... 0

Scores

						Score
						Weight
						Value = ▭

Jan	Feb	Mar	Apr	May	Jun	Jul	Aug	Sep	Oct	Nov	Dec	
												Goal
												Actual

Step 4.

Establish goals.

Your goals should be

- specific;
- challenging;
- measurable.
- realistic;
- attainable;

Then enter your goals into the matrix at the level corresponding to the score of 10 (see below)

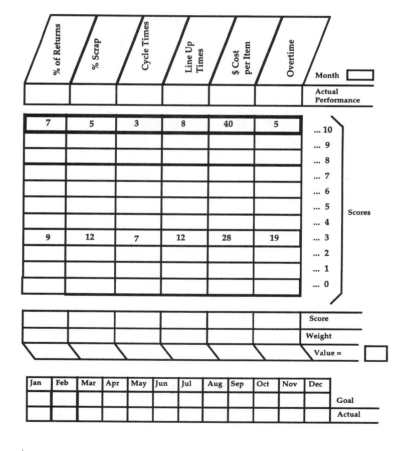

Step 5.

Establish mini-goals.

You will not be able to improve from a score of 3 to 10 overnight. It may take you a year to do this. Therefore, it is important that you are able to track your progress towards the final goal. Mini-goals will help you measure your improvement.

These mini-goals are entered in the matrix at the levels corresponding to the scores of 4, 5, 6, 7, 8, and 9, as below.

% of Returns	% Scrap	Cycle Times	Line Up Times	$ Cost per Item	Overtime	Month ☐
						Actual Performance

% of Returns	% Scrap	Cycle Times	Line Up Times	$ Cost per Item	Overtime	Scores
7	5	3	8	40	5	... 10
3	6	3.5	9	38	7	... 9
4	7	4	9.5	36	9	... 8
5	8	4.5	10	34	11	... 7
6	9	5.5	10.5	32	13	... 6
7	10	6	11	30	15	... 5
8	11	6.5	11.5	29	17	... 4
9	12	7	12	28	19	... 3
						... 2
						... 1
						... 0

						Score
						Weight
						Value = ☐

Jan	Feb	Mar	Apr	May	Jun	Jul	Aug	Sep	Oct	Nov	Dec	
												Goal
												Actual

Step 6.

Establish the lower performance levels.

Record the lowest possible level of performance. This allows any decline below your current performance level to be captured.

% of Returns	% Scrap	Cycle Times	Line Up Times	$ Cost per Item	Overtime	
						Month ☐
						Actual Performance
7	5	3	8	40	5	... 10
3	6	3.5	9	38	7	... 9
4	7	4	9.5	36	9	... 8
5	8	4.5	10	34	11	... 7
6	9	5.5	10.5	32	13	... 6
7	10	6	11	30	15	... 5 **Scores**
8	11	6.5	11.5	29	17	... 4
9	12	7	12	28	19	... 3
10	13	8	12.5	27	21	... 2
11	14	9	13	26	23	... 1
12	15	10	14	25	25	... 0

						Score
						Weight
						Value = ☐

Jan	Feb	Mar	Apr	May	Jun	Jul	Aug	Sep	Oct	Nov	Dec	
												Goal
												Actual

Step 7.

Assign weights.

Decide on the relative importance of each of the chosen indicators, then assign them a weighting. These weights should add up to 100 percent. (This weighting, multiplied by the score, will allow the team to calculate its overall performance for each period.)

% of Returns	% Scrap	Cycle Times	Line Up Times	$ Cost per Item	Overtime	
						Month ☐
						Actual Performance

						Scores
7	5	3	8	40	5	... 10
3	6	3.5	9	38	7	... 9
4	7	4	9.5	36	9	... 8
5	8	4.5	10	34	11	... 7
6	9	5.5	10.5	32	13	... 6
7	10	6	11	30	15	... 5
8	11	6.5	11.5	29	17	... 4
9	12	7	12	28	19	... 3
10	13	8	12.5	27	21	... 2
11	14	9	13	26	23	... 1
12	15	10	14	25	25	... 0

						Score
15	20	10	10	30	15	Weight
						Value = ☐

Jan	Feb	Mar	Apr	May	Jun	Jul	Aug	Sep	Oct	Nov	Dec	
												Goal
												Actual

Step 8.

Allow for a period of development.

Wait a month or two before confirming the final scores. During that period

- confirm that current performance levels are a fair reflection of the starting point;
- establish that the data for the chosen indicators are easy to collect;
- devise the simplest way to collect accurate data;
- confirm that the weighting is a fair reflection of the mission;
- develop a plan for the maintenance of the system and for data collection.

Step 9.

Plan for improvement.

Develop action plans that will improve performance in all areas. Ensure that these actions

- are spread over a reasonable period — so that you do not try to do too much too quickly;
- are things you have control over;
- have the support of your immediate supervisor.

Step 10.

Tabulate scores and calculate the index at the end of each period.

At the conclusion of each monthly period, you should gather data and plot the results on your chart.

- Calculate the actual measure for each productivity indicator and enter it on the performance line of the matrix.
- Circle the actual performance level achieved for each indicator on the scale. If a mini-goal is not achieved, the lower performance level should be circled. Any performance level lower than 3 gets 0 for the period.

- Score the corresponding performance (1–10) and enter it on the score line of the matrix.
- Mulitiply the weighting factors by the score to get a weighted value. Enter the totals on the value line of the matrix.
- Add the weighted values together. The sum should equal the performance index for that monitoring period.

Review your performance with your boss regularly. Send her a monthly copy with any appropriate comments.

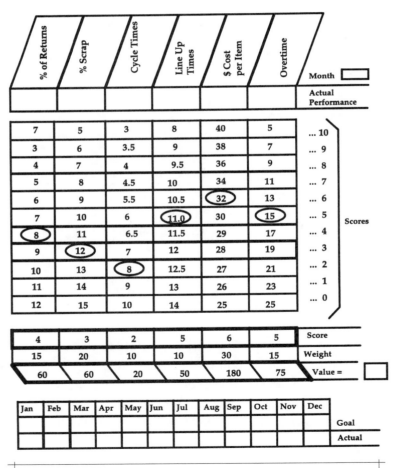

Step 11.

Plot the results.

The performance should be plotted on a graph against a target curve that starts at 300 and ends at 1,000, as below. A three-month moving average may be used to accommodate variations.

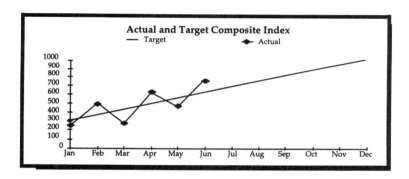

Meetings

$\mathcal{W}$hen he observed yet another huddle at a football game, George Will, the columnist and broadcaster, quipped, "It combines the two worst things about American life: it is violence punctuated by committee meetings."

There are more than 20 million business meetings each day in North America. Most people dread meetings because they are unproductive. But for teams to be effective, they need to meet in order to share information, solve problems, make decisions, and plan improvements.

Learning to run great meetings will make you a natural team leader. You will also earn the eternal gratitude of the attendees! Here's what you can do to improve your meetings:

BEFORE THE MEETING

1.
- Ask yourself if the meeting is necessary or if there is a better/ easier way of achieving your objective.
- Plan your agenda. Your meeting plan should state the purpose, items, length, and process.
- Invite key people only. People who don't have an interest in or knowledge of the subject matter will throw you off track or slow you down.

- Send the agenda to participants a few days in advance to give them time to prepare.
- Book a meeting room early and make sure it has all the needed equipment.

AT THE MEETING

2.
- Get organized. Ask one person to keep time, another to keep the minutes, and a third to record key ideas on a flip chart.
- Confirm the objective, time, and process. Get agreement on these items.
- Work through the agenda item by item. Make sure that each item is complete before moving to the next.
- Encourage attendees to stick to one topic at a time.
- Establish ground rules (code of conduct), especially if the meeting content is likely to inflame passions. For example, the group might agree to
  - listen to one another;
  - respect all ideas;
  - give everyone a chance to express opinions;
  - make decisions by consensus.
- Post these ground rules where everyone can see them.
- Appoint a "sergeant at arms" to help you enforce the rules, if necessary.
- Stay on track. If people begin unrelated discussions, remind them of the objectives. If necessary, offer to put an item on the agenda for the next meeting or deal with it at the end of the current meeting, time permitting.
- Pass out supporting materials only when the related item is being discussed. If you provide materials at the start of the meeting, participants tend to read them and get distracted from the agenda.

- Keep everyone involved. Ensure that everyone has the opportunity to participate, and that no one dominates the discussion.
- Keep the meeting flowing by asking lots of questions, such as:
  - How does everyone feel about that?
  - What's next on the agenda?
  - Are there any other opinions on this?
  - Can we move to the next item?
  - Have we all agreed to this?
  - How much time do we have left?
  - How will we deal with this issue?
- Ensure that each decision has an action before you wrap up the meeting. Ask for a volunteer to complete each item by a specific date. ASAP is not a specific date — it merely indicates that the activity will be done sometime in the future.
- Summarize the conversations at the end of the meeting so that everyone is clear about what has been covered.

AFTER THE MEETING

3.
- Send minutes to each person. Also post them on your bulletin board for others to see.
- Remind each person who has committed to do something of that responsibility by highlighting those action items in his or her copy of the minutes.

Meetings

Attending Other People's

$\mathcal{I}$f you are going to take the time to attend a meeting, make it worth your while and show respect to your chairperson by taking an active part. Here are some ways to make your participation meaningful:

BEFORE THE MEETING

1.
- Read the agenda. If the purpose of the meeting is not obvious, try to get the goals clarified before it takes place. If there is no agenda, suggest that one be established, either before or at the beginning of the meeting.
- If you are short of time, find out from the chairperson whether you are needed for the whole meeting. If not, arrange to be present during the relevant portion only.
- Find out how long the meeting is supposed to last, and tell the chairperson how much time you have available.

AT THE MEETING

2.
- Be punctual.
- Sit where you can make eye contact with the chairperson. This will give you an opportunity to participate fully and play an

influential role in any decision-making process.

- Be enthusiastic. Offer to take minutes, be the flip-chart recorder, or play some other useful role. Your commitment will be appreciated and emulated.
- Do your part to keep the meeting brief. To achieve this
  - glance obviously at your watch during overlong discussions;
  - offer to be timekeeper for each agenda item;
  - signal the chairperson if the meeting is falling behind schedule;
  - bring items to a conclusion by summarizing them;
  - ask if there are other items still to be covered;
  - ask if you need to stay for the remaining agenda items;
  - press for a decision on the item being discussed.
- If the meeting becomes bogged down in endless discussion, request that someone make a summary or ask whether the points have not already been discussed.
- Help others stay focused. If people go off on tangents, tactfully note that they are off topic or ask that that matter be dealt with at another time. Avoid participating in distracting side discussions.
- Be considerate of other points of view. Your colleagues will appreciate your respectful attention to their ideas.
- Avoid confusion by asking for clarification. Ask someone to summarize the discussion or conclusions so that everyone will have a good understanding of what's going on.
- Ask again for a summary, preferably by the chairperson, at the end of the meeting. Such a summary should make clear what the meeting achieved in relation to its objectives.

Meetings

How to Keep Them Short

$\mathcal{A}$ meeting should go on for only as long as it takes to reach its objectives. Typically, this takes much longer than it should. Here's how you can shorten your meeting time dramatically:

BEFORE THE MEETING

1.
- Ask yourself if the meeting is really necessary. If not, find an alternative, more efficient way of achieving your objective.
- Be clear about the objective. If you are not clear about what you want to achieve, no one else will be and the meeting will drift aimlessly.
- Make sure that the people who need to be present to make decisions can attend. If they can't attend, reschedule the meeting.
- Inform people in advance of the objective and agenda. Ask them to come prepared to deal with agenda items.
- Prepare an agenda. This document should
  - state the objective(s);
  - identify each step in the meeting;
  - indicate how long each item will take.

2.
- Start meetings on time. Don't wait for latecomers.
- Get agreement on the objectives and the agenda items at the start.
- Allocate specific times for each item on the agenda. This will allow you to better manage if certain items exceed their expected time allocation.
- Ask for a volunteer to be timekeeper. Ask that person to let you know if you are falling behind on any particular item on the agenda.
- Establish a "Parking Lot" on your flip chart. If issues unrelated to your meeting are brought up, ask if they can be recorded in the Parking Lot and addressed later. Typically, when an idea is recognized, the person bringing it up will let go of it.
- Avoid repetition of ideas by recording them on a flip chart.

3. Other strategies to the keep meetings short:
- Run stand-up meetings on the shop floor or in the office to avoid wasting time getting to meeting rooms. People will generally want to sit after standing for more than fifteen minutes, so they will be less likely to drag out discussions.
- Hold your meetings at the end of the day, scheduling them to wrap up at the official end of business. People will be motivated to finish on time.

Meetings

$\mathcal{A}$chieving your meeting objectives will be easier if you manage the people involved. A variety of behaviours will be demonstrated in any meeting, but there are many ways to deal with each.

1. Dealing with aggressive behaviour can be tough. Strategies to use include:

- Remaining calm. Showing anger allows the aggressors to feel that they have successfully caused you to lose your composure.
- Allowing people to vent. If someone wants to discuss a problem that is not on the agenda but that he needs to get off his chest, let him vent for a short while. If his issue is legitimate, albeit off topic, show empathy by agreeing. When he is finished, ask if he is done, and if so whether you can proceed with the topic at hand.
- Avoiding giving people a political platform. Don't allow people to use your meeting for their own political agendas. If someone's tone of voice is hostile and she begins to hijack your meeting, intervene when she stops for breath and point out firmly but politely that the matter may be important but that this is not the meeting at which it will be addressed.
- Avoiding debates. If a person is totally out of line, making

exaggerated claims or suggesting ridiculous ideas, don't debate with him. Canvass his peers to confirm that he alone holds that view. If there is general agreement that the hostile person's argument is invalid, confirm this by saying, "Well, it looks like no one agrees with you, so why don't we agree to discuss this later?" Then move on to the next item on the agenda.

- Finding out the reason for a person's anger so that you can deal with it inside or outside the meeting. If the person feels that you empathize, even though you cannot solve the problem, she will be more inclined to co-operate. This can be done within the meeting, if the issue is relevant, or outside, if it is not.
- Taking the person aside at a break or at the end of the meeting. Share your observations and frustrations. Ask for help in making the next meeting productive.

2. You can bring out the best in quiet or withdrawn people if you:
   - Invite participation by maintaining eye contact and directing questions at them periodically.
   - Use the person's name when asking questions so no one else can answer.
   - Ask questions the person should be able to answer to encourage self-esteem.
   - Sit opposite the quietest person so that your conversation can be directed to him.
   - Make quiet people feel useful. Give them jobs that will increase their visibility. The role of recorder will ensure that the person is standing up while canvassing ideas from the group.
   - Use a round robin to collect ideas. This technique gives everyone a chance to express an idea. People who don't have one can pass.
   - Get opinions on issues by asking questions that require a yes or no response. Praise people without appearing patronizing if they expand on their ideas.

- Give people advance notice of subjects to be dealt with in the meeting so they can collect their thoughts.
- Canvass their ideas one on one outside the meeting. If necessary, express those ideas to the group, giving due credit for it.

3. If someone tries to dominate your meeting, you can use many of the same techniques you use to deal with shy people. But they must be used in reverse. For example:
- Sit next to the person and keep eye contact to a minimum.
- Look at everyone but the dominator when posing questions to the group.
- Point out the problem, outside the meeting, while expressing your appreciation for the input. Ask for help in keeping everyone involved.
- Interject when the person stops to catch breath. You can say, "Thank you. What other opinions are there?"
- Indicate your desire to get a variety of opinions before you ask a question.
- Get opinions in sequence (round robin), reaching the dominant person last.

4. If someone tries to sidetrack your meeting, you can:
- Post the meeting objectives where they can be seen by all. Before the meeting begins, get agreement to stick to the agenda.
- Point to the objective on the wall and ask if people could focus their comments on the central meeting purpose.
- Ask how the issue is related to the subject under discussion.
- Interrupt when the person takes a breath, with a comment such as "Thank you, but it appears that we are on to something else. Could we agree to get back on topic?"
- Allot a "Parking Lot" on a flip chart to record issues unrelated to the meeting. Agree to deal with these issues later.

Meetings

Keeping Minutes

*M*eetings are never isolated incidents. They are part of an ongoing process of information-sharing, problem-solving, decision-making, and planning. Proper documentation can help ensure that decisions are not forgotten and that actions are followed up. This is how it can best be done:

1. Ensure that you have a secretary either before or at the start of the meeting. This person should be someone other than the meeting facilitator, since it is unlikely that one person can do both tasks properly.

2. Confirm that the secretary knows how to record the minutes. Minutes can be very detailed, noting differences of opinion on each issue and attributing them to specific individuals, or they can be a summary of what was discussed and agreed upon. The latter approach works best in most situations (see example below).

3. The secretary should record
   - the time and place;
   - the objectives;
   - attendees;

- absentees;
- key discussion points;
- decisions that were made.

4. At the end of the meeting have the secretary summarize to ensure that notes accurately reflect what happened.

5. The secretary should ensure that all actions indicate who will undertake them, when they will be done (specifically, not ASAP), and who needs to be informed.

6. After the meeting, circulate the minutes. Send them to people who are affected by the decisions taken.

7. Minutes can be a communications tool. Post them on a bulletin board for all interested people to read.

Mentor

Finding the Right One

Mentoring is about giving gifts —
gifts of confidence, encouragement and respect.

ELIZABETH HOYLE, TRIMARK INVESTMENTS

*W*hen Odysseus embarked on his long journey in *The Odyssey*, he chose his wise friend Mentor to guard, guide, and teach his son, Telemachus. All of us can benefit from having someone to help us. But picking the right person is key, so that the end benefit will be achieved.

Not every smart, articulate, experienced person makes for a perfect mentor. Picking or being matched with the wrong person will produce limited results. In fact, the outcome could even be a career-limiting experience as your mentor might badmouth you in the organization. To the extent that you can choose your mentor, find someone who meets all or most of these criteria:

1. Finding someone to mentor you successfully can take time. An ideal mentor will be someone who:
- Does not work in your department. Find someone who can bring a whole new perspective to you, someone with different technical skills and work experiences.

- Is more experienced than you. This usually goes with age, but not necessarily so. A person with experience will have moved between jobs, organizations, and industries. This will have given her more varied experiences. She will have made more mistakes and, it is hoped, has learned from them.
- Is senior to you in the organization. This will enable him to bring a larger perspective to you, one that often escapes people "in the trenches."
- Is humble. A humble person is not a know-it-all. Such a person is prepared to think before talking. Better still, she would look to you to answer some of your own issues rather than giving you the answer all the time and expecting you to "buy" it without question.
- Facilitates problem-solving by acting as a sounding board. He is concerned with your growth. Therefore, he makes you think about answers and alternatives. When asked for answers, he throws the ball back to you with questions such as "Well, what do you think?" or "What are some of your options?"
- Thrives on other people's successes. This person cares about you. She celebrates and finds joy in your achievements.

2. Ideal mentors are people who
   - are great role models;
   - listen more than they talk;
   - enjoy learning from their protegés;
   - care about and value the relationship;
   - have a great attitude — are positive, upbeat, and optimistic;
   - care about honesty (they know how to give feedback that is frank and focuses on the problem, not your personality);
   - are tolerant (they accept you for who and what you are without wanting to change you).

Mentoring

Managing Your Relationship

The older I grow, the more I listen to people who don't say much.

GERMAINE G. GLIDDEN

You are the protegé. Your mentor has kindly given of his or her time to help you. But statistics show that most formal mentoring relationships are not successful — as many as a third end in the protegés leaving the company. Be one of the successes. Here's how:

1. Get the relationship off to a good start. Get involved in selecting the right mentor. Don't be passive and accept anyone "given" to you.

2. Be assertive if you feel there is a mismatch. It's better to pull the plug on the relationship at the outset instead of struggling to maintain a relationship that has little value to either party.

3. At your first meeting, come prepared with clear objectives and an agenda. Key things to discuss are:
   - *Your needs.* Are you looking for help with your career? Developing political savvy? Improving your knowledge about the industry? Make sure that your mentor is the best person to help you.

- *Your expectations of the mentor.* Do you expect that person to be a fountain of knowledge, a friend, a sounding board, an advocate, an observer, or some combination of these?
- *The frequency and length of meetings.* Will the meetings be one on one, by phone, during or after work hours?
- *Boundaries.* Set up guidelines that will make clear the things that are inside or outside the relationship. Issues of confidentiality are important. Also, will you confine yourself to business issues, or can you cover issues outside work? And what about honesty? How frank will you be with each other if either party does or says something that the other considers offensive?
- *Length of the relationship.* Most relationships last about a year. What are the expectations of each of you?

4. The ongoing relationship will be effective if you
   - meet your commitments;
   - respect the time constraints of the mentor;
   - confine yourself mostly to the issues with which the mentor is best placed to help you;
   - do not betray confidences of other people to the mentor;
   - show your appreciation to the mentor, particularly if she or he has gone out on a limb for you in some way;
   - give polite but assertive feedback if you feel the mentor has betrayed your confidence in any way.

5. If the relationship is failing to add value and both of you are struggling to find things to discuss, it may be time to call a halt to the meetings. If so:
   - Be frank with the mentor. He or she will probably be grateful.
   - Show your appreciation. A small gift or a lunch is appropriate.
   - If you have been part of a formal mentoring program, send a note to the program coordinator stating your appreciation.

Mistakes

*The key competitive strategy is for a company
to learn from what it does.*

JACK WELCH, GENERAL ELECTRIC

*Y*ou're probably human if you make mistakes. All humans do. But we don't all deal with them appropriately. If you have done something wrong, here are some suggestions on how to handle the situation:

1. Accept your own mistakes. You may be frustrated and disappointed with yourself, but there is no point in exacerbating the situation by looking for a scapegoat elsewhere.

2. Accept that mistakes are part of life. You will always make them. In fact, the busier you are, the more you will make.

3. Evaluate the situation. Ask yourself specifically:
   * Does it impact others?
   * How big is it?

4. If it's a local mistake that doesn't affect anyone else, and you know how to fix it, do so. No need to tell the whole world.

5. If the problem impacts others, fix it if you can and tell whoever needs to know, pointing out what you've done to fix it or what you will do. You can also suggest how you will prevent it from happening again.

6. If you can't fix the problem, find someone who can. Make notes on the solution so that you'll be able to prevent it from happening again or will be able to fix it yourself if it does happen again.

7. Since the people affected by your mistake may be clients — internal or external — let them know you are sorry. That may take some of the anger out of them.

8. If you ever make a mistake that will embarrass your boss, make it known to her right away, with an apology and the corrective action. Never let her find out from doing detective work or hearing through the grapevine. She will regard you as untrustworthy and monitor your performance more closely than you will like.

9. If you make a mistake and can't figure out how to fix it or avoid it the next time, get help. Approach people collaboratively and ask for their ideas. By explaining your problem to someone else, you will often arrive at a solution yourself. If other advice is useful, thank the person who has given it.

10. Learn from your mistakes, especially the larger ones. Make changes immediately so that the new skills and behaviour become part of your everyday activities.

Money

How to Earn More

*S*ome people say that money is a motivator. It is not. But when you feel that you are underpaid, you can become demotivated. Everyone likes to feel appreciated, and getting a fair and competitive salary will make you feel good about yourself. Here are some tips on how to improve your earnings:

1. Find out where you stand, compared with the average. You can do this by:
   - Asking for this information from your salary administrators. If they are reluctant to divulge this information, ask them to refer you to any industry studies.
   - Asking friends and associates within your organization and in similar jobs in other organizations for their salary rates. Make sure to compare apples with apples. Include all benefits in your comparison.

2. If you find that you are over the fiftieth percentile — in your job category and in the industry — you need not rest. You may be good enough to get the eightieth percentile . . . or better. So at your next performance review:

- Review previous commitments. What goals did you set? What training did you intend doing? What commitments had you made that would result from the training?
- Go to the next appraisal armed with a list of specific accomplishments — big or small. Make sure that they are included in the documentation.
- If you have been poorly evaluated in some areas, ask why, and ask for advice on how to do better.
- Negotiate a performance incentive. Tie your compensation to a measurable goal that appeals to your boss. In that way, you've created a win-win situation.

3. Never be afraid to discuss money with your boss. If it bothers you, and you feel you're undervalued, make your case; but do so courteously. Most important, be armed with the facts, not opinions. Show
- how you compare with others;
- what you've done that's special;
- how your last increase related to inflation.

4. If you feel that you have lost track of your goals, refocus. Let your boss know that you're back on track and what you're doing to achieve your goals.
- If your goals are general — such as to improve customer service — make them more specific. A goal to improve turn-around of customers' questions by 17 percent by the year end is specific.
- If you feel you are unfairly paid, make your boss aware of your opinion. Don't demand a raise. Take a collaborative approach. Ask for your boss's help and advice. Say, "I'm not sure what to do about this. What advice would you give me?" Then listen and note any specific action steps.

5. Keep your ear to the ground to identify things that are important to the organization. Keep up to date on new programs. Get involved. Become part of a design team or an information-collecting task force. These steps will increase your profile and place an added value on your employment.

6. Be nice. Be positive. Be friendly. People will go out of their way for special people. You'll have people advocating for you if you're well thought of.

7. Be especially nice — without being patronizing — to people in power. They can negatively influence your career if they don't know you or don't care for you.

8. Act like an employer. Treat the organization as if it were yours. Love it. Take care of it. You'll earn few, if any, kudos if you act like an employee who plays strictly by the rules, does the minimum, goes home as early as possible.

9. Keep your ears and eyes open for new opportunities. Watch the bulletin boards for job openings. Apply for those that might challenge you. Have a plan to show an interviewer how you intend to make a success in the new role.

10. Review the mission of your organization. Get hold of the business plan. Find out what's important so that you can align your efforts with what is valued by senior management. For example, focus on
    - generating higher sales;
    - opening new accounts;
    - reducing costs.
    Measure these changes and share them with your boss.

11. Tackle with gusto problems that have been unsolved. Show that you are a "can do" person. Summarize your efforts in writing to your boss.

12. Improve your education. Go for improved qualifications or a higher degree. Show your boss how the additional education will benefit the organization — you may then get the company to fund you.

13. Become indispensable. Learn a niche skill, such as how to operate a new software package, that adds to your value.

Negotiating

Win-Win Tactics

Don't ever slam a door; you might want to go back.

DON HEROLD

*No power is strong enough to be long lasting
if it labours under the weight of fear.*

CICERO

The outcome of a negotiation can be win-win, win-lose, or lose-lose. Sometimes you strive for a win-lose, such as when you buy a car or a home (it is hoped that you win and the seller loses). But at work, a win-lose attitude with your boss or peers will come back to haunt you. You might win the first round, but sooner or later the loser will get even! Here's how to produce a mutually beneficial result:

1. Before you begin formal negotiations
  • Develop a list of alternative outcomes. Evaluate them all. Select the best plus some acceptable fall-back positions that could still meet your needs.
  • Prepare yourself thoroughly. This will reduce your stress level and give you an ability to display confidence.

2. At the start of your negotiations

- Establish a joint goal. Even if the parameters are broad, you and your colleague will both focus on the objective instead of beating each other up.
- Establish ground rules for the negotiations. This is particularly useful if the negotiation has typically created conflict and emotional outbursts. You might both agree to
  - listen to each other without interruption;
  - respect each other, even though you may disagree on issues;
  - be flexible on the less important issues.
- State your needs clearly and firmly. Make sure that the other party understands them by getting verbal confirmation.
- Determine the other person's needs. If you can meet his needs, chances are he will meet yours. If you frustrate him, he will do the same to you. Find out what his needs are by listening. Focus on what he is telling you instead of on formulating rebuttals. If you are not sure, ask him to repeat himself, or paraphrase his words to confirm understanding.

3. During the negotiations

- Find common ground and build on it to solve other problems.
- Prioritize issues. Determine what is negotiable and what is not.
- Try to understand what people think and feel. Read their non-verbal language. What are their facial expressions telling you? What are their eyes doing when you ask for commitment? What are their postures and hand gestures telling you?
- Avoid arguing, especially on minor issues. Train yourself to agree to the small things so that you establish a collaborative environment focused on solving the more important items.
- Avoid aggressive behaviour. Such behaviour will result in a win-lose outcome. The behaviour is typified by

- talking louder than the other person;
- dominating the discussion;
- using sarcasm;
- using authority (if you have it) to force the other party into acquiescence.
- Avoid passive behaviour. This behaviour is characterized by
  - an unwillingness to deal with the issues;
  - failing to make others aware of your concerns.
- Behave assertively. Be hard on the issues, but soft on people.
- Avoid blaming others. Otherwise you poison the atmosphere and cloud the focus.
- Always give your reasons for declining a proposal.
- Realize that the past can't be undone, and dwelling on it will cause hostility and defensiveness.
- Look to the future. Visualize how much better things will be if both parties are able to get satisfaction.
- Probe. Ask questions. Listen carefully. In this way, you will uncover the needs of the other person. By finding those needs and then meeting them, you will set the stage for having your needs met.
- Show positive body language. Don't
  - fold your arms or legs;
  - roll your eyes;
  - tense your body;
  - wear a scowl;
  - raise your voice.
- Seek creative solutions that satisfy both parties. This happens more often when you:
  - Avoid "either/or" solutions. Limiting yourself to two alternatives reduces the possibility of creative new solutions.
  - Use the words "what if" more often.
  - Focus on common interests rather than opinions.

- The party with the shortest deadlines will tend to concede more as the deadline approaches. If you have a deadline, don't reveal it.
- Deal with issues as they arise so that they don't accumulate and overwhelm your discussion.
- If your negotiations are going off on a tangent, get back on track with a comment such as "Yes, I can relate to that, but could we get back to the central issue?"
- Be creative. There is more than one way to reach your goal. Have alternative ideas that will still provide benefits for all. Rigidity reduces creative problem-solving and increases conflict.
- Stop negotiations from time to time to share your feelings. Find out how others are feeling. If they are negative, find ways to overcome the hostility so that you can continue to solve problems in a constructive manner.
- Whenever the discussion becomes vague, clarify your understanding with a summary. For example, say "Do I understand the problem right? In my mind, it is . . ."
- In a unionized environment, be aware of items affected by the collective agreement. These should not be negotiated on a one-to-one basis.

4. At the conclusion of the negotiation
- Avoid making extra concessions during the euphoria of reaching an agreement with the associate.
- Summarize everyone's understanding so that everyone is absolutely clear as to what has been agreed upon. Commit it to paper so that no one will have to rely on memory for the details.

Networking

Associate yourself with men of good quality
if you esteem your own reputation;
for 'tis better to be alone than in bad company.

GEORGE WASHINGTON

*M*ore contracts are granted, and more jobs won, based on contacts. You need to develop strong marketing skills that leave an indelible impression on the people with whom you come into contact. Networking successfully is both a science and an art. You can improve your chances of successfully impressing people if you:

1.   Open your horizons. Consider the world your market. Take opportunities to network wherever you are — in the supermarket, in a line at the cinema, and, of course, at professional gatherings. You never know who you will meet, or what connections they might have.

2.   When you're in a room full of strangers, here are some ways to network successfully:
   • Initiate discussions. Make small talk. Find something that you have in common — impatience at waiting, the same sneakers, books, etc. Behave in a friendly manner. Display a happy, warm

disposition. Observe people's reactions to you and respond accordingly. If the initial reaction is negative, try someone else. If it's positive, go beyond.

- Have a "grabber" punchline always ready. It should be something that positions you as worthwhile, smart, or inquisitive but never boastful.
- Find out and use people's names. Do a quick association so you won't forget it, and then use it a few times in the first minutes.
- Display your curiosity about the things others do and what interests them. Probe them for details beyond the superficial.
- Learn to describe what you do in simple terms. Make it sound interesting. Act enthusiastic when you describe your activities.
- Ask lots of questions to establish a link that may be of value to you. Try to find an item to trade so you can help your new contacts in some way. This will motivate them to pursue the discussion.
- Dress appropriately. When in doubt, dress up. Always appear neat and clean.
- Smile a lot. Stand tall. Project enthusiasm, but with warmth and sincerity.
- Shake people's hands at the beginning and end of your conversations with them. Make this firm, but not a bone-crusher. Add a couple of seconds to the shake with people with whom you feel you have connected, to give them the subtle reinforcement that you have placed a value on your meeting.
- Relax and be yourself. Don't try to project something you are not.
- Divulge something unusual about yourself to try to pique their interest in you. Show that you are different, special, and unique in some way.
- Share business cards. Find something on the person's card that is worth talking about. Say things like "Gee, that seems interesting. Can you tell me more about that?"

- Avoid bragging or name-dropping. Behaving with humility is far more attractive than putting yourself on a pedestal.
- Avoid excessive eating or drinking — you will be sending a signal that you are somewhat overwhelmed by the situation, as opposed to appearing to fit into the situation like a glove.
- Make it easy for people to use your name. Display your name appropriately, and add a smiley face or some interesting sticker to attract attention and help get the conversation going.
- Ask lots of open-ended questions, rather than questions that can lead to a yes or no response.
- Listen to others. Be patient. Encourage people to talk so that you can pick up clues to the things they need and want. By tailoring your message to their needs, you will get yours met more often.
- Be positive. Think of three to six adjectives that apply to you both personally and professionally. This could include adjectives such as decisive and driven, which might set you apart. And be prepared to back your description with anecdotal evidence.

3. Keep up to date with the newest ideas in the industry. Know how they work, what they do, and how you can use them. If possible, develop some experience with them so that you can speak authoritatively.

4. Network constantly. Look at every gathering as a chance to expand your network. Talk to people at your church, in the bank line-up, on the bus. But be sensitive to people who may not want to reciprocate. Back off immediately if you sense that people have little interest in pursuing the discussion.

5. Set a goal for expanding your connections each week. Keep a log. If you have a computerized system to collect a list of contacts, categorize them so that you can refer to them quickly.

6. Follow up with people on things you offered to do for them or things they undertook to do for you.

7. Join committees where people of like minds and interests will be found. Volunteer for projects, particularly if there is a likelihood that you will work with people who can assist you.

8. Keep new connections in a file. Categorize them. Keep in touch with key people by sending them cards on holidays. Or send them little thank-you notes if they give you some help.

9. Finally, treat networking as a game. Make it fun. Challenge yourself to see how many contacts you "win" and how many you "lose." Set goals for a win-lose ratio or for the number of new people you want to meet each month.

Paperwork

Reducing the Clutter

$\mathcal{T}$he explosion in the use of computers made some people suggest that we would create paperless workplaces. The opposite is now evident. Attaching printers and copiers to computers has made the duplication of information so simple that the amount of paper we are using has increased dramatically. Here are some things you can do to reduce the waste and save yourself lots of time too!

1. Attack your desk! Put all the papers you see around you into one pile. Then go through them, one at a time, and choose one of these options for each:

- File it. Get it out of sight. File it in a place where you can retrieve it without any problems.
- Handle it. Make a decision. Respond to the person who sent it to you. Delegate the word processing to someone else if possible, or simplify the process by writing your reply on the letter and faxing it back.
- Refer it if you are not the best person qualified to deal with it.
- Throw it out. Most of the papers lying on your desk probably fall into this category; they've been around for so long that they have no value any more, or they are fun things that you thought you might have a use for but no longer do.

2. Improve your filing system. You need the peace of mind that will enable you to retrieve information when it's out of sight. So don't

- Create files that are described by an adjective, adverb, date, or number. For example, you're unlikely to find your Hot Prospect or New Products file, but you will find something in Prospects. Use nouns for file titles.
- Create new files for every person or topic you hear of. Combine them. For example, Customers' Needs and Quality Service files can be combined under the heading Customer Service.

3. Shorten your reports. It will reduce the time you need to create them and save your reader time. Key strategies are to

- add pictures and graphs instead of narrative;
- include details and tables in the appendix, in case people want to refer to them;
- include an executive summary outlining the issue, solution, plan, and benefits;
- use bullet points wherever possible.

4. Reduce the number of reports printed. If people ask you for a copy of a certain report, ask them why they need it. Perhaps they don't. Maybe one section only will suffice. Or perhaps they need a different report.

5. If you are on a circulation list that includes people who don't even work in your organization, think about removing your name. The information is probably redundant. Or, in the unlikely event that you need a copy at some time, you can track down that one issue.

6. Reduce your reading of

- corny solicitations;
- forms that are duplicated;

- letters sent to you to cover someone's behind;
- reports and letters that have just about the entire organization on the "cc" list;
- reports that are as heavy as a brick, but that contain only one page of interest to you;
- policy manuals that are so detailed they would make you an indentured servant were you to follow all their directions.

Performance Review

Getting

*Perfection is achieved not when there is nothing left to add,
but when there is nothing left to take away.*

ANTOINE DE SAINT EXUPÉRY

*U*nfortunately, the performance review (or appraisal) has become a standard feature of organizational life. It's unfortunate in that managers rely on it to provide annual feedback to people who need it daily. Since the appraisal often influences a person's salary and also his or her career, it is very important. Here are some suggestions on how to make it work for you:

1. Make notes of your issues and concerns with the process as described or as you know it.

2. Identify ways to deal constructively with the flaws in the process. For example, if you are not given a copy of a questionnaire to complete beforehand, ask your boss if this can be done. Also, if you are not given notice of the meeting, ask your boss to give you a few days to prepare.

3. Keep notes in a file of all issues that have had a bearing on your performance through the year. These should include
  - special projects you have participated in;
  - special achievements;
  - your goals and actions you have taken to achieve them;
  - courses you have taken and uses you have made of the program content;
  - any special recognition given to you by people other than your boss.

4. Collect your thoughts on
  - training you feel would help you and the organization;
  - where you could get this training, its dates and costs;
  - your career aspirations;
  - things that frustrate you at work and how you would like to deal with them;
  - things that frustrate you with which you need help;
  - new projects you'd like to do;
  - new responsibilities you feel you could undertake.

5. If salary issues are dealt with during the survey, try to find out
  - where you stand in the range of salaries;
  - if there is room to move to a higher grade;
  - what the organization's policy is regarding compensation, particularly when compared with similar organizations, and at what percentile does it want to position itself;
  - what co-workers are being paid.

6. At the meeting, ensure that the process is collaborative. While you should be prepared to clear up misconceptions and misunderstandings assertively, it's important that you are collaborative. Spend most of the time

- listening;
- making notes;
- summarizing;
- asking questions.

7. At the end of the meeting, thank your boss for her feedback. Thank her for her help if the process was useful and care was taken. Summarize your understanding of agreements. Make sure that they are written down.

Planning

*Within all of us there is an elusive melody
which when heard and followed
will lead us to the fulfillment of our fondest dreams.*

SIEGFRIED AND ROY

Planning is the conscious process that enables us to decide how to go from where we are to where we want to be.

1. Planning helps us
   - define our goals;
   - decide to make changes;
   - know what to change and when to make the changes;
   - measure our progress;
   - identify roadblocks that might prevent us from being successful.

2. A proper plan brings with it benefits, which include having
   - a direction to follow;
   - a clarification of the road ahead;
   - a coordinated effort to reach a goal.

3. Many people fail to plan because
   - the process requires them to commit themselves to action;
   - they have a fear of failure;
   - the plan is leading them into unfamiliar territory, which may unnerve them;
   - they lack the ability to visualize anything better;
   - they have a history of unfinished tasks and are afraid to go down the same road yet again;
   - they feel an inability to be more spontaneous.

4. There are a number of steps to take in developing a plan:
   - Decide what you want. Close your eyes and picture yourself and your situation in the ideal, completed state. Write down what it is you want.
   - Evaluate where you are. Be realistic. Answer these questions:
     - What is happening now?
     - Who is influencing the situation?
     - When do these problems occur?
     - Where am I now?
     - Why am I in this situation?
     - How are things currently being done?
   - Assess how large the gap is between your existing situation and what it is that you want to achieve.
   - Identify any roadblocks that will prevent you from being successful. Categorize these roadblocks as follows:
     - Class 1 — You have full control to deal with them.
     - Class 2 — You have partial control to deal with them, and so you may need some help.
     - Class 3 — You have no control and are most unlikely to remove this roadblock.

- Evaluate your chances of success. As long as the obstacles are of the Class 1 and 2 types, you should be able to succeed. However, tackling goals that have Class 3 roadblocks can lead to failure at worst or only partial success at best. Be realistic. Modify your goals or abandon the project.

5. Get help to overcome Class 2 roadblocks. Don't try to deal with them yourself.

6. Identify the major milestones that will lead you to your goal. Set them out in the order they should take place.

7. Decide on and document the minor steps you need to take.

8. Set target dates for major milestones and minor actions.

9. Prioritize key actions that will lead you to your goal.

10. Document your plan. Use one of a variety of methods such as pert charts, Gantt charts, or action plans.

11. Review your plan with others who have been down the same path that you intend to travel.

12. Take the first step to achieve your goal. Reward yourself for starting.

13. Monitor your plan to make sure you are achieving each milestone on the way to ultimate success.

Politics in the Office
A Survival Guide

We can't look out for number one because there is no number one. The world is a team.

RON MCCANN AND JOE VITALE, *THE JOY OF SERVICE*

*O*ffice politics is characterized by infighting, power plays, hidden agendas, manoeuvring, and pettiness. If unchecked, it can have disastrous consequences on morale and an organization's ability to meet its mandate. Here are some guidelines to help you cope:

1. Recognize that no organization is free of politics. It is an inherent part of organizations.

2. Understand that it is difficult to remain neutral. It's like being in a battlefield. If you're in the middle, trying to pick up bodies, you could get hit by the crossfire. It's better to learn how to play the game smart, so that you either win more often or survive a loss.

3. Before you commit to enter a battle between two opposing camps, consider the following:
- Pick your battles. Don't get involved in every issue. Pick those that give you a good chance of being on the winning side.

- Get a sense of what senior people are thinking. Look at issues from their perspective and join the side that aligns with real power-brokers.
- Only fight battles you're likely to win. Don't fight against large odds, senior people, or large numbers unless the issue is of major philosophical importance to you and you're prepared to lose your job because of it.
- Make sure you have allies who will stand with you and defend your position. The more senior the people in your "posse," the more energy you can put into the conflict.
- Have some empathy for the other side. See things from that point of view. Maybe there is more than one way of doing things. This way, you'll spend time on issues of real difference, instead of appearing petty on all issues.
- Look for common ground. Often our differences are semantic but not fundamental.
- Take the big-picture perspective. In the overall scheme of things, how important is the issue you are fighting for? Learn to let go of issues that are not important, or trade favours so you can win some battles too.
- Maintain a sense of humour; it often breaks the tension and allows people to collaborate more readily.
- Reduce your personal criticism of others, focusing more on issues. It's easy to fault others and just as easy for them to fault you.

4. If you notice faction fights developing, consider these strategies:
- Avoid joining a faction that is trying to bring down your boss. This is unethical and could easily backfire on you.
- Avoid taking a position that is contrary to the interests of the organization.

- Consider getting off the boat if you feel your faction is about to lose. But don't get into the opponent's boat — it's probably time to be neutral and lie low for a while.
- Fight important battles hard. But also fight fair. Don't resort to unethical practices — they'll come back to haunt you.
- Form alliances of your own with like-minded people. This will promote the longevity of your relationships. Teaming up with people whose values differ from your own will require you to compromise yourself and your principles.

Presentations

I and mine convince not by argument, smile and rhyme –
we convince by our presence.

WALT WHITMAN

Opportunities to make presentations are increasing in number. Even if you are not in management, you could be called upon to make a presentation as part of a task force that is recommending a change, a work team that is reporting its results to management, or your own desire to sell a significant new idea. This section will show you how to get ready for a presentation and how to conduct it with maximum impact.

1. Before your presentation, you should:
- Research the members of your audience. Find out what their "hot buttons" are.
- Prepare thoroughly. Make sure you have supporting documentation. For complex presentations, prepare information packages for each attendee, preferably distributing them ahead of time.
- Choose your visual-aid medium. Slides or overheads are suitable for a formal presentation; a flip chart can be used for more informal events. Visual aids can reduce comprehension time by about 40 percent.

- Plan to accommodate the different types of learning styles:
  - visual;
  - auditory;
  - kinesthetic.

  Your presentation will have the greatest effect if it includes all three forms.
- Plan your agenda. It should cover:
  - welcome and introductions;
  - objectives of the presentation;
  - description of the problem;
  - explanation of the solution;
  - benefits to your audience;
  - your action plan;
  - your methodology in reaching a conclusion;
  - question-and-answer session;
  - request for permission to proceed;
  - wrap-up.
- Prepare your visual aids (slides or overheads). Remember to
  - keep them short and concise;
  - have no more than one idea per slide or transparency;
  - use pictures wherever possible;
  - keep lettering large and legible.
- Plan the verbal part of your presentation, keeping it short (fifteen to twenty minutes). The simpler the proposal, the shorter the presentation should be. Use the KISS principle. (Keep It Short and Sweet).
- Do a dry run. Get your information all together and pretend you are facing your audience members. Imagine their reactions. If you tape-record your performance, you will be able to gauge where to improve the presentation and your timing.
- Create an emergency kit of supplies you might need during the presentation. These could include markers, masking tape,

projector bulbs, pens and pencils, and name cards.
- Invite the audience members well before the presentation, and confirm their attendance shortly before.

2. On the day of the presentation, you should:
- Get there early. Make sure that the equipment you need is there and that the seating is set up appropriately.
- Try the view from different parts of the room to make sure that everyone in your audience will be able to see the projection screen and/or flip chart.
- Check the equipment and do a test run with the slide or over-head projector to make sure it works and to get comfortable with it.
- Make sure you have spare projector bulbs. Murphy's Law ensures that a bulb will burn out during a key part of your presentation if you don't have a spare one.
- If your audience members will be seated at tables, set up a place for each person, with name card, agenda, and paper and pen, if appropriate. Do not, however, hand out your written material until your spoken presentation is over. Otherwise your audience will be reading instead of listening.

3. During your presentation, you should:
- Welcome your audience members with confidence and warmth as they arrive. Greet them with a smile and a relaxed handshake.
- Welcome attendees officially after all have sat down, and out-line your plans for the meeting, including breaks, if any. Let them know they will receive copies of your presentation at the end. If the presentation is taking place away from their normal workplace, also direct your audience to washrooms and emergency exits.

- Make sure your listeners know how you intend to take questions, whether at the end of the presentation or as issues arise. The latter approach will demonstrate both confidence in your material and consideration for those attending.
- Keep to your agenda, making clear which item you are dealing with and when it has been completed.
- Begin with a bang. Use a human-interest anecdote to get your audience emotionally involved, or offer a radical challenge that will pique listeners' interest.
- Use rhetorical or actual questions to keep your listeners feeling part of the presentation. Periodically ask for a show of hands on a particular issue. Challenge your audience.
- Pay the most attention to members of your audience who are likely to give constructive feedback during question-and-answer sessions, thus putting you in a positive light (*see also* Meetings: Managing People).
- When faced with a long-winded, rambling question, ask if the questioner can summarize the gist in about twenty words (*see also* Meetings: Managing People).
- Paraphrase questions so that the entire audience can hear them. This will also give you time to think about your answer.
- Use answering questions as a means to restate your important points.
- Avoid trying to answer a question when you can't. Either poll the audience for someone who does know the answer, or offer to get back to the questioner when you have had a chance to check the information.
- Prevent hostile audience members from railroading your presentation by
  - avoiding a defensive stance;
  - refusing to engage in argument;

- using humour, especially during tense moments;
- focusing on facts rather than opinions;
- polling other members of your audience for their opinions;
- offering to deal with their concerns, preferably outside the meeting, especially if they are off topic (*see also* Meetings: Managing People).

- Keep the presentation short and concise. Don't bore your audience by dealing with information they know — focus on new material.
- Avoid insulting your listeners by reading to them from your written presentation or visual material. Give them a few seconds to absorb each slide and then paraphrase it to emphasize your main points.
- Keep your presentation moving smoothly with "bridging" remarks between slides or overheads.
- Maintain eye contact with the audience. To increase audience contact:
  - Scan your listeners, looking at each for a few seconds. Concentrate on those who seem to be responding positively; this will increase your confidence.
  - Never turn your back to read from or describe something on the screen. You will be hard to hear and could lose your audience.
- Keep your audience interested:
  - Vary the pace of your presentation.
  - Change tactics every five to seven minutes. Different approaches include asking questions of your listeners, doing a poll, getting the audience to fill in a form or questionnaire, setting up group activities, etc.
  - Modify your speech. Change the volume, speed, and tone of your voice from time to time, especially when you are about to make an important point.

- Use animated facial expressions and gestures.
- Make assertive (not aggressive) gestures at key points. These could include pointing a finger, punching the air, or using familiar signals from sports.
- Keep moving. Standing stiffly behind a podium may make you feel safer, but it will set up a barrier. Walk around the room, getting closer to your listeners during questions. You will find that the activity will release tension and make you feel more in tune with your audience.

AFTER THE PRESENTATION

Use this list to evaluate how well you did. It will help you identify areas to improve on next time. You should be able to answer yes to all the questions.

	YES	NO

Did you:
- Thank your audience for attending?
- Distribute and follow an agenda?
- Get everyone's agreement on the length of the meeting?
- Introduce the benefits of your proposal at the beginning?
- Keep it short and simple?
- Avoid dwelling on details?
- Project confidence?
- Vary your visual aids?
- Speak without using notes?
- Use a deliberate tone of voice?

AFTER THE PRESENTATION (CONTINUED)

YES   NO

Did you:

- Move around the room?
- Keep eye contact with listeners?
- Thank everyone who helped?
- Focus on the positive?
- Finish on schedule?
- Request support?
- Involve your whole team?
- End with a summary?

Presentations

Using Visual Media

*P*resentations that include a visual component are far more memorable than ones that are merely spoken. Here are some ways to give impact to your visual material:

1. When using a flip chart, remember to:
  - Write main points in heavy capital letters.
  - Use broad-tipped pens in dark colours — black and dark blue are best.
  - Reserve lighter colours for highlighting, underlines, bullets, numbers, etc.
  - Avoid solvent-based markers. They can give some people headaches and tend to bleed through flip-chart paper.
  - Distinguish headings by making them larger, underlining, or using a different colour.
  - Use one page for each separate idea. If you have made up pages before the presentation, place tape "divider tabs" on the sides of the sheets so you will be able to find them easily.
  - Have small pieces of masking tape ready (keep them on the legs of the flip-chart stand) to post important sheets on the wall. This will keep key ideas in front of your audience.

- Besides writing down key points, use the flip chart for diagrams such as plans, flowcharts, and organization charts — anything that will increase your audience's understanding.
- Remember: a picture is worth a thousand words. Use one whe ever possible.

2. Slides and overheads use many of the same principles that flip charts do. You need to remember to:
- Check the equipment before the presentation, especially to see if the light bulb is working. Some machines have two — check them both, and make sure you have replacement bulbs.
- Try out the equipment beforehand so you can get used to how it operates. Different brands of projectors have different switching and focusing systems.
- Make sure the picture is in focus, straight, and filling the screen as much as possible.
- Clean the lens and the face plate of the overhead projector, to avoid having dirt specks on your picture. Make sure your slides and transparencies are clean as well.
- Transparencies are easy to mix up. Number them and lay them out in order in front of you so you can see what's coming next. This will help you make bridging comments between overheads. Plain paper between the transparencies will help you see what's on them and will also protect them from scratches.
- Keep projected written material very short and simple. Slides and transparencies should follow the 4-by-4 rule: no more than four lines each, and no more than four words per line.
- Avoid using your finger to point out items on an overhead transparency. Any shaking from nervousness will be magnified and will distract your audience. Use a stir stick or a flat-sided pencil that won't roll off the projector.

- If you plan to mask items and discuss them one by one, let the audience see all the information first. (This of course does not apply to answers to questions or surprise elements.)
- Be careful not to block your audience's view. Remember the people at the sides of the room.

Problem-Solving
Creativity Using Brainstorming

Great ideas, it has been said, come into the world as gently as doves. Perhaps then, if we listen attentively we shall hear, amid the uproar of empires and nations, a faint flutter of wings, the gentle stirring of life and hope.

ALBERT CAIRNS

Imagination rules the world.

ALBERT EINSTEIN

Problem-solving requires creativity, but most adults, as a result of negative feedback while growing up, have lost the majority of their creative ability by age forty.

1. Problem-solving is something you do all the time. When the problem affects a number of people and it is complex, it is best to get the affected people together to solve it. This way, you're likely to have two benefits:
   - The solution will probably be better than any one person can come up with.
   - You will have commitment to its implementation.

2. Call a meeting of people who have an interest in solving a particular problem. Here are things to do in preparation:
- Warn people about the meeting at least a week in advance so they have time to think about the subject.
- Plan to get a variety of ideas by inviting people with different backgrounds and diverse skills to add fresh perspectives.
- Include in your group at least one person with the reputation of being a maverick.
- Choose a location. The more informal and unusual the environment, the more creativity you can expect.

3. Your meeting will be successful if you do these things:
- Before the meeting starts, get people into a creative and relaxed frame of mind with an icebreaker.
- Restate the purpose of the meeting. Indicate your desire to encourage new ideas.
- Appoint a recorder to write all ideas on a flip chart.
- Use brainstorming to generate ideas. Explain the rules of brainstorming:
  - *Quantity.* Get as many ideas as possible. Don't worry about quality.
  - *No discussion.* Discussing issues will reduce the number of ideas. Leave discussion and comment until afterwards.
  - *No criticism.* Don't judge ideas. Early evaluation will stifle the development of unusual ideas.
  - *Record.* Record ideas on a flip chart, where they are visible.
  - *Piggyback.* Build on ideas. A ridiculous idea might spur a very practical idea from someone else.
  - *Incubation.* If you run out of ideas, leave your list and return to it later. You will usually find that participants have more new ideas.

- Conduct a round robin. Ask people to call out their ideas one at a time, in rotation. Those who don't have ideas can pass.
- Keep the process moving quickly. When you sense that ideas are drying up, encourage contributions from anyone, rather than by rotation.
- When all ideas have dried up, revisit the list so the team can piggyback. Use these ideas to spur new ones.
- If you are dissatisfied with the ideas on your list, give the group more time to incubate. Collect more ideas after a break or a few days later.
- Only when all ideas are exhausted should you refine the list. Eliminate duplications. Evaluate ideas based on criteria such as
  - payback period;
  - novelty;
  - cost;
  - benefit;
  - ease of implementation.

Problem-Solving

The Team Approach

Opportunities multiply as they are seized.

SUN TZU

$\mathcal{M}$ost adults are good problem-solvers. They deal with tough issues daily. But each person has a different process for dealing with life's challenges. So when people get together as a team and they don't have a common process, they are bound to head for conflict. To make the process easier, here are some ideas to help you and your team through it:

1. Identify a problem to work on from such sources as
- customer complaints;
- observations of poor work practices;
- data-collection systems.

2. Form a team. Pick people who
- have an interest in the problem;
- are impacted by the problem;
- will make time to resolve it;
- have the power to implement a new solution.

3. Establish ground rules for the team. These could include an agreement to
   - listen to each other;
   - respect a variety of ideas;
   - start meetings on time;
   - maintain a focus;
   - ensure that no one dominates the discussion.

4. Get agreement on how the team will operate. Decide
   - how often you will meet;
   - how you will communicate with each other between meetings;
   - how you are to be organized (i.e., what roles are necessary and who will fill each);
   - what tasks are to be done by each person;
   - what deadlines the group faces.

5. Define the problem (*see the* Problem-Solving Road Map on page 249) on paper, being as specific as possible. For example, instead of broadly defining a problem as a "lack of communication," narrow it down to a "lack of communication between the first and third shifts." An effective way of defining a problem is to answer these questions:
   - Who is responsible?
   - What happens?
   - When does it happen?
   - Where does it happen?
   - How does it happen?

6. Investigate the cause. Your team has two options: it can rely on people's opinions or on data. Data are preferable, particularly when issues are complex and emotional. Opinions are acceptable for less contentious or urgent problems.

7. Find solutions. Brainstorm for innovative ways to resolve the problem. At this stage, creativity is essential (*see* Creativity). Consider all the possibilities and then pick solutions that can be implemented quickly and cost-effectively.

8. Develop an action plan. List all steps to a solution, then get members to take responsibility for implementing the ideas by a specific date or time. Do not accept ASAP — it's too vague and means that the activity probably won't get done!

9. Implement the plan. Give the volunteers your go-ahead and then follow up to make sure each person understands his or her mission.

10. Complete the problem by
   - measuring the outcome;
   - tracking the benefits;
   - recognizing the team;
   - evaluating the process.

11. Evaluate the process with your team. Identify those things you did well so you can repeat them for other problems, and correct the things you could have done better.

Problem-Solving

The Top Ten Principles

*Most people would rather die than think;
in fact, they do so.*

BERTRAND RUSSELL

*O*rganizations grapple with the same problems year after year, wasting incredible amounts of time and money. The reason for their failure to resolve problems is the lack of a process. Using simple principles, you can resolve problems quickly and effectively. Here's how:

1.   Prioritize problems. Deal with key issues first. The 19th century Italian economist Alfredo Pareto taught us to differentiate between the critical few and the trivial many (later known as the 80/20 rule).

2.   Focus on problems over which you have control. Problems can be classified into those over which you have
   - full control;
   - some control;
   - no control.

3. Clean up your own backyard first. Don't look for problems in other areas until *you* are perfect! Your own problems usually can be fixed the quickest. Then go on to problems that require the co-operation of your boss or the people in the next department. Do not get frustrated about problems over which you have no control. Leave them. If they really bother you, bring them to the attention of senior management and then get back to solving your own issues.

4. Follow a step-by-step approach. Problem-solving is most effective when it follows a sequence of steps (see the Problem-Solving Road Map on page 249). Without such an approach, people often start with solutions. Don't jump to conclusions or try to solve problems before defining them or finding their real causes. This wastes time and money, since the solution might not remove the root cause.

5. Rely on data whenever possible. Facts are always more compelling than opinions. Unless the problem is small or insignificant, collect statistics to provide answers to the five *W*s and an *H*:
- Who is causing the problem?
- What is causing the problem?
- When does it happen?
- Where does it occur?
- Why does it happen?
- How does it happen?

6. Break the problem down so you can deal with one aspect at a time. Problems having to do with quality, communications, and productivity can be enormous and may defy solution. To reduce their impact, deal with these problems in the same way that you would eat an elephant: take one bite at a time!

7. Use a team approach where necessary. Remember, many hands make light work. The greater the involvement and contribution of others, the more the commitment to implementing the solution.

8. Involve people who are part of the process. Every organization is staffed with people anxious and willing to solve problems, and they bring a variety of talents to team problem-solving. Use them. Don't try to do everything yourself; you'll become a dumping ground for problems. Some people are
- good at detail work and can collect data accurately;
- creative and can find ingenious new ways of doing things;
- good at group process and able to develop team spirit and resolve conflict.

9. Don't be bound by an old paradigm. There is a lot of conventional wisdom about how things should be done. Sweep it away! Look for new and innovative solutions. Brainstorm (*See* Problem-Solving: Creativity). Get lots of ideas, even wacky ones. Build on some, combine others. Then decide on the best. The more unconventional the idea, the more you might be inclined to pilot it. After a successful test, implement it across the board.

10. Get a fresh perspective on old problems. Get the opinion of new employees. Since these associates are not stuck in existing paradigms, they probably have new ideas for solving old problems.

PROBLEM-SOLVING ROAD MAP

STEP 1: DEFINE THE PROBLEM
State the opportunity succinctly.

STEP 2: FIND THE CAUSE
Investigate all possibilities. Narrow down to most likely.

STEP 3: FIND SOLUTIONS
Be creative. Look for alternatives. Pick the best.

STEP 4: PLAN IMPLEMENTATION
List actions, dates, and who will assume responsibilities.

STEP 5: IMPLEMENT
Carry out actions according to plan.

STEP 6: MONITOR
Measure progress.

Productivity

*Most people like hard work, particularly
when they're paying for it.*

FRANKLIN P. JONES

An efficient workforce is a productive workforce, whether it is producing goods or providing services. Productivity is a crucial element of competitiveness. Here are some ways you can help your organization be more productive:

1. Examine how you are spending your work time. What percentage of it are you using for activities that relate directly to your objectives? If it's less than 95 percent, you may have a problem.

2. Set clear goals in consultation with your boss. If you supervise other staff members, share your goals with them. Break your goals down into individual objectives for each staff person.

3. Measure your and your staff's progress towards goals, recording and posting them for visual reinforcement.

4. Encourage your colleagues to monitor their own productivity so they will gain an increasing sense of responsibility for their performance.

5. Keep alert for new ideas that will help you and your colleagues work more efficiently, and then encourage their implementation.

6. See that people receive recognition for good ideas. Share any that you come across so that all the members of your team can benefit.

7. Do an evaluation of important processes on a regular basis, involving others who are part of the process. Everyone should document all the steps in his or her part of the process on a "map" (*see* Reengineering Work Processes). Evaluate each step with the following questions:
   • Is this step necessary?
   • Does it duplicate other steps?
   • Does the step add value?
   • Does the step cause delays?

8. Concentrate on doing a job right, not quickly. Haste causes mistakes, which may make it necessary to do the job all over again. This can lead to poor service and lower productivity.

9. After you have found the best way to do a job, document the process and share your findings. If you have responsibility for other staff members, make sure they are trained to do the job correctly. Promote the most efficient procedures.

10. Support the idea of cross-training in your organization, and be the first to volunteer for training opportunities. Cross-training creates a more flexible team of workers who can substitute for or help each other when people are overloaded, sick, or on vacation.

11. Before you decide you need to replace a manual task with a machine-run one, work to make the process as simple and efficient as possible. Automation for its own sake can sometimes *decrease* productivity.

12. Avoid unnecessary meetings. Try to get business done through informal stand-up sessions in the office or on the shop floor. Keep these to five or ten minutes.

13. Reconsider your paperwork. Ask yourself these questions:
  - Is anybody reading it?
  - Does anyone need the information?
  - Are the data it contains useful for making decisions?
If you answered no to any of the questions, work to simplify or eliminate the task.

14. Organize your workspace and areas shared with other staff members. Make sure things can easily be found, preferably by keeping them in full view. This will help avoid time-wasting searches.

15. Benchmark what you do. This will help you compare
  - performance indicators that can be measured;
  - methods and procedures.

16. Compare what you do with
  - similar work areas in your organization;
  - similar work areas in other organizations;
  - different work areas in other organizations.

17. Be receptive to new ideas, even if they come from very different workplaces, and you will discover new opportunities. For example, you might discover how to reduce customer line-ups in a bank by comparing how hotels process lines of people at checkout time.

18. Adapt new ideas to fit your work situation.

PRODUCTIVITY: QUESTIONS TO STIMULATE IMPROVEMENT

Look at processes in your workplace with your colleagues. Ask yourselves these questions to discover new ideas for improving productivity.

— Is every step in this procedure necessary?
— Does every step add value for our customers?
— Are there steps missing?
— Who checks work while it is being carried out and when it is finished — the people who do the work or someone else?
— Does the process have a logical workflow?
— Where are the significant delays in this procedure? What is causing them?
— Are people who do related activities stationed near each other?
— Do certain policies and procedures prevent improvements?
— Are people empowered to make improvements in their own jobs?
— Have we any data on our productivity?
— Are productivity data shared with the entire workforce?
— Can we involve more people in seeking out ideas to improve productivity?
— How necessary are the improvements we have made?

Project Management

The Top Ten Principles

Crisis is another name for opportunities.

ANONYMOUS

*M*urphy's Law postulates that if anything can go wrong, it probably will. It is the rare project that finishes on time and within budget. But with proper planning, committed people, well-defined goals, and strong sponsorship, you have a good chance for success. Managing the middle and end of your project is particularly important.

1. Before your project begins, get organized and be clear about what you are getting into.

- Get a clear mandate and make sure it is well documented, especially if the project is large. The mandate should
  - be clear and unambiguous;
  - define the parameters of the project;
  - indicate whether you are to research, recommend, or implement change.
- Be sure that the parameters of the project make clear:
  - The geographical scope. Will the project cover a part or all of your organization, one city, a province, or the whole country?
  - Which departments will be involved, and how. Who will

participate and who will be affected? What responsibilities will each have to the project?

- Your authority. What powers do the team and its members have? What are their spending limits?
- Which levels of the organization will be affected.
- Which products or services are included in the project.
- Which systems or processes are included.

• Ensure that your committee or team represents every part of the organization that will be affected by the project. Team members should have

- time available to devote to the project;
- skill and experience in working in groups;
- knowledge of the subject;
- an assortment of viewpoints.

• Plan carefully. Document the steps to be taken, when they will occur, who will carry them out, and how they will be done. Get your sponsor to endorse the plan.

2. Start the project well. At the first meeting:

• Welcome the attendees.

• Explain the mandate and goals of the project, review the parameters, and ask for comments and further explanations.

• Together with your teammates, establish ground rules for behaviour. Some examples:

- We agree to finish our work on time.
- We agree to be on time for meetings.
- We agree to be honest with each other.
- We will respect the ideas and opinions of our teammates.
- We will give the team leader advance notice if we cannot complete a task on time.

• Present your plan, specifying tasks, target dates, and responsibilities. If everyone cannot agree to the plan, work with the team to modify it until they do. For large or complex projects, it is best to develop the plan from the beginning as a team. This will result in more commitment to goals from team members and a better plan.

- Anticipate obstacles that could prevent the plan from being completed on time and within budget. List them in order of importance and get team input on how to remove or avoid road-blocks. If necessary, get volunteers to deal with these items by a defined date (not ASAP).
- Remind team members of the benefits they will receive, however intangible, from successful completion of the project.

3. Keep the process on track:
- Monitor progress, especially of tasks that are critical to the success of the project.
- As project manager, avoid doing any of the work yourself. Leave the technical aspects to team members — if they are falling behind, replace them or get extra help. Don't get caught up in details; you will lose sight of the big picture.
- Give frequent progress reports; they are essential for team morale. Let all team members know about successes so they will feel pride in their achievements.
- Give recognition to team members who outperform expectations, and let their bosses know about their contributions to the project.
- Stay within your parameters as defined at the outset of the project. If you feel the need to go beyond the parameters, negotiate a change in them first.
- Stay focused on your goal. If your project has more than one goal, make sure everyone on the team knows which are the most important.
- Set a standard of professional behaviour for the project. Be a role model by

- staying out of politics, especially in other departments;
- focusing on problems, not people;
- refusing to criticize people who are not team members;
- running top-quality meetings that begin and end on time, include all team members, and cover an agenda that you have distributed beforehand.

THE TOP TEN WAYS TO GET ANY PROJECT TO REACH ITS CRITICAL MASS

1. Put in ten times as much effort as you think it should take (ten inputs for every one output).
2. Bring in three partners, advisers, friends, or colleagues, and let them advise and support you.
3. Package the project so that it adds *extraordinary* value to the consumer, not just the customer.
4. Take consistent but learned action every day or week. Press forward, regardless.
5. Motivate yourself and others by creating a visual display showing measurable progress.
6. Bring in customers/users and alpha testers at the very beginning and *learn* from them.
7. Link the project to your vision. When both are connected, the project gets a big lift.
8. Maintain a healthy reserve: twice as much capital/expenses/time as estimated.
9. Force the project to prove itself, in some way, during each stage of its development.
10. Once you've done all of the above, *then* trust your gut.

Re-engineering
and Downsizing

Life After Change

*I am a lone monk walking the world
with a leaky umbrella.*

Re-engineering and downsizing are usually thought of as the same thing. They are not. Downsizing is typically an ill-conceived attempt by people in power to pander to shareholders or the public to reduce costs. It is an admission of failure — failure to continuously fine-tune an organization to keep it fighting fit or lean and mean. Re-engineering is about examining work processes and finding innovative ways to eliminate waste, duplication, and non-value-added activities. It can result in significant quality improvement, as well as time and cost reduction. But often it requires changes in organization and work habits.

1. If your organization is being downsized, you can do little other than

- pray;
- stay positive;
- update your resumé;
- appear to be busy.

2. If your organization is re-engineering its work processes, volunteer to be involved. In this way, you can participate in the analysis of existing workflow and have some input into the changes that will result.

3. After a re-engineering investigation or a downsizing exercise, expect the following to happen:

- Initially, there will be sighs of relief from people who are not directly impacted.
- There will be a feeling of guilt on the part of people who survived, particularly if close working friends were laid off.
- Confusion will set in as work arrangements and responsibilities are changed.
- Some will feel resentment at having larger workloads. Passive-aggressive behaviour, rather than outright challenges, can be expected.
- Supervisors will run around like chickens with their heads cut off. They will carry more of the slack until they are able to delegate assignments.
- Monitoring of performance will increase, as it is expected that people will improve their performance as a payback for having kept their jobs.
- Stress will go through the roof.
- The number of resignations will increase.
- Eventually, things will settle down and return to more normal conditions.

Re-engineering
Work Processes

*Y*ou're in the business of satisfying your customers. Studies show that one of the primary reasons for losing customers is slow service. Doing things right and doing them fast are really important. Yet studies of most work processes will indicate that they are hopelessly inefficient. In fact, the processes usually add value only 5 percent of the time. In other words, 95 percent of the time the process is at a standstill.

By mapping out work processes, you have a magnificent opportunity to identify waste and duplication. Changes — when significant in size and scope — will enthrall your client and reduce frustration on the part of the people providing the service.

1. Identify a process that can be improved significantly. Pick a process that

- is causing customer frustration and complaints;
- could save significant dollars if improved;
- relates to the departmental and corporate mission;
- is relatively simple to solve;
- can yield a measurable improvement.

2. • Form a team. Invite six to ten people to help you improve the process. The team should represent all stages of the process and

include people from two or more departments. Select people who
- understand the process;
- are concerned about improvement;
- will make the time to work on the team;
- have the power to make changes.
- If your team consists of front-line people, you will need a mandate from a senior manager to make changes. Such a mandate will give participants the feeling that their hard work will not be in vain.
- Hold your first team meeting. At the kick-off you should
  - introduce members to one another;
  - explain the process and the steps you will be taking;
  - train people in the tools of process-mapping;
  - get commitments from all members regarding their participation.

3. Map the process. Give people a week to collect information from the perspective of their work areas. Invite them to a meeting at which you will map the process.
- At the next meeting, record all the steps of the process on a white board. The board should be pre-drawn with the names of the people who are involved on the left and the time on the bottom (see page 263).

Example of a Process Map

- Note the opinions of participants as you guide them through the steps of the process. Record activities, starting on the left side and moving to the right. Write each activity or decision on a Post-It Note. The advantage of a Post-It is that it can be moved easily. If you are unsure about any part of the map, leave it blank and continue. You can do detailed research later.

- Use appropriate symbols for each step in the process. The most commonly used icons are:

Process Mapping Symbols

Activity

Decision

Document

Delay

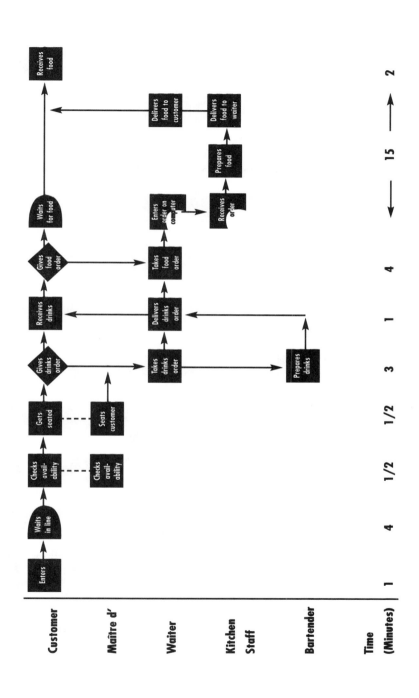

Customer	Enters	Waits in line	Checks avail-ability	Gets seated	Gives drinks order	Receives drinks	Gives food order	Waits for food	Receives food
Maître d'			Checks avail-ability	Seats customer					
Waiter					Takes drinks order	Delivers drinks order	Takes food order	Enters order on computer	Delivers food to customer
Kitchen Staff								Receives order	Prepares food	Delivers food to waiter
Bartender					Prepares drinks				
Time (Minutes)	1	4	1/2	1/2	3	1	4	15	2

- The process map should show
  - each step;
  - the inputs and outputs of each step;
  - all decisions;
  - the people involved;
  - the time needed to do each step.
- Create a draft drawing of the process and allow team members an opportunity to confirm its accuracy with their peers.

4. Analyze the process.
  - At your next meeting, adjust the process based on feedback from team members.
  - Ask the team:
    - Is each step necessary?
    - Is the flow logical?
    - Does each step add value?
    - Are some activities missing?
    - Are some steps wasteful?
    - Is there duplication?
  - List the problems. Prioritize them based on their impact on the customer, their cost, and their time requirements.
  - Deal with the major problems primarily by developing action plans to improve them.
  - If the process is inefficient, consider scrapping it and starting anew. You can establish new ways of improving the process by considering one or a combination of different options:
    - *Outsourcing*. Research whether some other organization can do all or some aspect of the process better, cheaper, or faster than can be done internally.
    - *Finding new technological solutions*. Are there new equipment, software, or Internet solutions that can be applied to improve the process?

- *Benchmarking*. Find other organizations who have similar processes that they do better and faster than you do. Find out how much better they do the process and how they achieve this.

5. Redesign the process. Based on the team's ideas, redraw the process map to reduce waste, duplication, and time.

6. Implement change.
   - Develop action plans for all the improvements.
   - Spread the changes among as many people as possible to ensure that the workload is evenly distributed.
   - Hold meetings with all those affected to make sure that they
     - understand the changes;
     - agree to the changes;
     - will make the changes.

7. Monitor and hold gains.
   - Follow up with people to make sure that the changes are being implemented.
   - Encourage and recognize efforts to reduce the difficulties usually associated with change.

8. Measure the results. Keep a tally of the improvements. Charting them and displaying them for everyone to see will promote pride in all those responsible. It will also increase enthusiasm for your next process-improvement project.

PROCESS IMPROVEMENT
ROAD MAP

STEP 1
Identify an opportunity.

STEP 2
Form a team.

STEP 3
Map the process.

STEP 4
Analyze the process.

STEP 5
Redesign the process.

STEP 6
Implement change.

STEP 7
Monitor and hold gains.

STEP 8
Measure the results.

Relationships
Developing Bonds with Co-workers

*It's more shameful to distrust one's friends
than to be deceived by them.*

DUC DE LA ROCHE FOUCAULT

*Y*our success is primarily a result of your initiative, hard work, knowledge, and skills. But it is also dependent on the people around you. They can choose to make your worklife pleasant, or they can strive to make it miserable. Developing good relationships with the people around you will be good for your mental health, stress level, and career. Here are some things you can do to build relationships:

1. Be courteous. Treat others with respect. Treat them as you would want to be treated.

2. Be empathetic. Understand people and their feelings. Put yourself in their shoes.

3. Be accepting. Don't waste time trying to change people. You can't. You can, however, change your behaviour towards them. You'll find people so much more receptive if you accept their beliefs, religion, colour, etc. After all, this is real power in diversity. Having everyone follow one line of thinking and beliefs is not only boring, but also downright dangerous. While you may not be enthusiastic about everyone's opinions, you must accept their right to have a different opinion.

4. Be patient. Don't rush to judgement. Think about what people say before making rebuttal statements.

5. Be kind. Do little things to show you care. It could be a gesture as small as getting a colleague a coffee while you are going to get yours or offering to help when your desk is clear. Don't expect reciprocity. You will get it back sooner than you think.

6. Be true to your word. Keep your promises. Meet your commitments. In fact, try to exceed people's expectations. Do things better and more quickly than expected.

7. Be responsive. Do things quickly. Returning phone calls is an area where you can demonstrate a commitment to reliability and speed.

8. Be appreciative. If a person is nice to you, acknowledge that. Don't take kindness for granted. Show your appreciation in ways such as:
   - Leaving a thank-you note on his desk.
   - Sending a card with a personal message.
   - Bringing him some baked goods to have with morning coffee.
   - Offering to help with a task considered tedious.

9. Be collaborative. Look for win-win situations. Focus your most competitive instincts outside your organization, not on your colleagues. Help people save face. Find some value for others in a solution. Try to compromise if the outcome is not significantly impacted.

10. Be open. Listen to new ideas. Listen to be influenced. Accept that there is more than one approach.

11. Be humble. Admit your foibles. Show that you are fallible. Don't sweep your mistakes under the carpet. Admit problems, but show how you will fix them.

12. Be helpful. Volunteer for tasks. Be first. Show the way. Show leadership. Take the initiative. Your great attitude will soon infect those around you. Try to stay positive, even when those around you don't respond; sometimes it takes a while for the infection to spread!

Relationships

Working with a Difficult Boss

*Y*ou seldom get to choose your boss. What you do get to do is influence how you work together. It is not the boss's job to make you happy. And since you spend more time being influenced by your boss than by people outside work, do whatever you can to make the relationship successful. Here's how:

1. Realize that you're unlikely to find the perfect boss.

2. View your relationship as a challenge rather than a problem. Make it your goal to develop an effective relationship so that work can move from the "drag" category to "tolerable" or even beyond.

3. Realize that your boss has significant power over you. He does your performance review and has greater access to the most senior people. There's little point in getting into a war with him: when you leave you may find it harder to get a new job as a prospective employer will want to check on your performance with your previous employer.

4. Become a problem-solver. Think about the problem from your boss's perspective. What are you doing that causes a problem? Fix your part of the problem without waiting for the boss to respond, because that's the area over which you have most control.

5. Avoid badmouthing your boss behind her back. You never know if your opinions will filter back. If they do, you'll land in hot water without having the ability to repair the breach of trust.

6. Avoid malicious obedience. Sometimes people do exactly what they are told to do, knowing that it will lead to failure. Don't embarrass your boss. Try to make things work, even if you don't agree with him 100 percent.

7. If your frustration is boiling over, set up a meeting with your boss to make her aware of your feelings. Key principles to remember:
   - Hold your meeting behind closed doors. A place away from work would be ideal. Consider taking her out for lunch, so the conversation can be done in a congenial setting.
   - Avoid using the word "you." Make the problem yours. Use "I" constantly. For example, say, "I am really frustrated when I have to change tasks before completion. Can you understand why this would frustrate me?"
   - Ask for any advice she can give to help you deal with your issues.

8. Let the boss know when he has done something new or different that has pleased you. Acknowledge his action with a show of appreciation — that way, he might be inclined to do more for you.

9. As a last resort, consider leaving. You might ask for a transfer within the company or quit the company altogether. If you do quit, you might be able to make a statement in an exit interview. Avoid the temptation to go overboard and blame your boss for everything. Try to be objective. Stick to the facts and do so professionally.

Safety

Taking Care of Yourself

_H_ealth-and-safety issues are everyone's business. Management may be legally liable for the accidents of its workers, but workers need to take care of themselves too. Accidents do happen. But here are some ideas for reducing and eliminating them:

_1._ Make health and safety a top priority. Let your people know how you feel about the subject, and what your mutual obligations are.

_2._ Deal with unsafe practices immediately. Make no exceptions. Allowing them to continue simply sets a dangerous precedent.

_3._ Get involved in finding ways to improve.

_4._ Find new and better ways of ensuring safety, even if you have the best record around. Keep yourself knowledgeable about current legislation and your role and responsibilities.

_5._ Always assume that whatever can happen will happen. Be pro-active. Anticipate possible accidents and prioritize them in terms of probability and severity. Establish guidelines for dealing with accidents.

6. Review your health-and-safety rules, especially when they change. They are usually available on a special bulletin board.

7. Share responsibility for health and safety with your team. Appoint a coordinator who can ensure that peers maintain safe practices. This person may serve on the health-and-safety committee.

8. Participate in departmental meetings to review problems, statistics, and procedures.

9. Spread ownership for health-and-safety issues by getting your workers to present a short related topic at each meeting. Your encouragement, plus a prize for the best presentation, might act as an incentive.

10. Beware of fatigue caused by excessive work demands. Fatigue reduces people's concentration and makes them more vulnerable to accidents. People can fall asleep or make mistakes that might otherwise not happen.

11. Learn the proper and safe methods of using machinery and equipment. If hazards are high, training needs to be thorough. Procedures should be documented and properly enforced.

12. Keep the environment as safe as possible and maintain good housekeeping practices: repair damaged flooring, improve inadequate lighting, and replace poorly constructed furniture.

13. Review near accidents. They are danger signals.

14. Report and record all accidents, no matter how minor. These statistics will help you analyze trends, pinpoint problems, and confirm the results of corrective actions.

15. Always have on staff an adequate number of people with current first-aid certification.

16. Use appropriate safety protection always, but remember that protective gear is a last defence against injury, not a replacement for safety. Always stop work when conditions are hazardous.

17. Encourage a team approach. Reward and recognize people for taking care of one another.

18. Help new employees to learn and practise safety. Make sure that they are fully briefed on your health-and-safety rules.

Self-Confidence

$\mathcal{S}$elf-confidence will make or break your career. People who feel good about themselves and their abilities will tend to
— take risks;
— volunteer for challenging tasks;
— voice their opinions at meetings.
These are the people who will do best. Here's how you can improve your self-confidence:

1. Give yourself daily affirmations. Say to yourself, "I'm terrific" or "I can do anything" when you get up or arrive at work.

2. Look in the mirror each morning and greet yourself with a smile. Tell yourself how terrific you are.

3. Reward yourself for achievement, no matter how small. Take a break, buy yourself an extra coffee or paste a motivational sticker on your equipment to acknowledge your achievement.

4. Complete all tasks, no matter how unpleasant they may be. And do them to the best of your ability. Then pat yourself on the back to confirm your grit and determination.

5. Ask for feedback from your boss and peers when you have completed a new task. Most people will be kind and will acknowledge your achievement.

6. Ask for regular informal feedback to confirm that you are on track. Don't wait for your annual appraisal to find out how you are doing.

7. Take every opportunity to learn new ideas and skills. Put them into practice quickly. Review the results.

Self-Development

*By nature, men are alike; by practice,
they get to be wide apart.*

CONFUCIUS

Weaving a net is better than praying for fish.

ANCIENT CHINESE PROVERB

*L*earning will improve your career and your self-esteem. Putting your learning into practice will be a tribute to your courage, ingenuity, and determination and will enhance the possibility of career advancement. Do these things to keep ahead:

1. Learn from successful people. Seek out these people and ask them to share their life secrets.

2. If successful people are not readily available, write down a list of people you admire. Go to the library and see if there are biographies and autobiographies on these people. Read them and see if you can glean the essence of their success. Make a list of these "nuggets" and prioritize them. Then take them one at a time and start to use them.

3. Identify people in your organization whose careers seem to be taking off. Observe them whenever possible. Try to sit in on their meetings. Volunteer to be on their task forces. Ask them for advice on how to improve your career.

4. Learn from mistakes. If you are human, you'll make many. And that's okay, so long as you don't keep repeating them. Think about what you did wrong and what you can do differently the next time, given the opportunity. When next in the same situation, do everything possible to try a new strategy. If it works, give yourself a pat on the back. If not, try Plan C next time.

5. Subscribe to trade journals. Find one idea you can use in each issue. Circulate the idea to show people that you are researching value-added ideas.

6. Take courses whenever they are offered, even if you've been on a similar course before. You'll always learn something new from a different instructor or from different approaches.

7. Access any funds available for training. Many organizations pay for programs outside work that can influence your performance.

8. Become a self-directed learner. Take responsibility to get information yourself. If you have a learning centre in your organization, visit it frequently. Find out what's new. Take advantage of Computer Based Training (CBT) during quiet times.

9. At the end of each workshop, summarize what you have learned and, more important, what you intend to do. Put theory into practice within a week. After that time, your memory and enthusiasm will fade fast as you get back into your old groove.

10. Avoid going to courses that run three to five days. There is too much to learn and too little time to put everything into practice. One- and two-day courses are better. They tend to be more focused and practical.

11. Avoid going to courses back to back. Spread your attendance over a period. This will give you time to digest the information and put ideas into practice, and then an opportunity to learn some more.

12. Focus on skills that will enable you to do things that the organization considers its highest priority. This will keep you in the limelight.

13. Buy books and borrow books. Don't read them cover to cover. Pick key chapters and skim them to get kernels of ideas. Read the summaries first to discover if the chapters are of interest.

14. Save time. Get summaries of books and tapes to listen to while travelling to and from work.

15. Speak to friends who have been to interesting workshops. Ask them for summaries. Borrow their workbooks, with references to key sections.

16. Go to conferences whenever possible. Seek out competitors. Buy them drinks at the end of the day and pump them for useful information about unique things they are doing.

Selling Your Ideas

Nothing can take the place of persistency.
Talent will not; nothing is more common
than unsuccessful men with talent.
Genius will not; unrewarded genius is a proverb.
Education will not; the world is full of educated failure.
Keep believing. Keep trying.
Persistence and determination alone are omnipotent.

CALVIN COOLIDGE

What's the point of having great ideas if you can't sell them to the people who control the green light to implementation? And if you never see your idea implemented, how much satisfaction will you derive? Here are some ways to increase the odds of getting approval for your project:

1. Before you meet with a potential sponsor:
- Be prepared.
- Pick your best ideas. Don't try to sell every one. Choose those that
  - are in line with the organization's mission;
  - have a reasonable chance of being accepted;
  - you feel passionate about.

- Collect as much information as possible to support your position. Facts speak louder than words.
- Find examples of similar ideas that have worked elsewhere. This will enable you to demonstrate a precedent.
- Don't rely on presenting your ideas orally. Collect them in documented form. This will add legitimacy to your position. Colour brochures of the equipment you want to buy or expert endorsements in credible trade or business magazines will all enhance your position.
- Make people aware that your idea could be used by a competitor. This may spur action that will keep you one step ahead.
- Be prepared to talk the language of your audience. If dealing with management, are you ready to show a cost-benefit?

2. When you are making your pitch:
- Greet the attendees warmly. Thank them for their time.
- Let them know your expected outcome. Be specific and assertive. Speak with a firm voice that emphasizes key results.
- Be positive. Saying "I expect to come away from this meeting with approval" is better than "Perhaps, maybe, you'll let me try it."
- Be optimistic, yet realistic. Don't exaggerate the benefits.
- Give attendees a chance to ask questions. Listen carefully to what they have to say. Answer them or offer to get back to them if the answer requires further thought or research.
- When your presentation is done, be silent. Don't speak. Wait till you get a "buying signal," such as "When can we start?" or "Do you think we can manage, given our lack of time?" Then assure them of success and show them your timetable.
- Avoid asking for approval in a way that allows them to say no. Replace "Can we go ahead?" with "Do you have other ideas that would ensure success?" or "When do you think we should start?"

Speeches

Preparing

Speeches are like babies — easy to conceive,
hard to deliver.

PAT O'MALLEY

$\mathcal{D}$oing your homework before a speech will improve the chances of your success dramatically. Here are some things you can do to be prepared:

1. Contemplate what you have to offer. Think about:
- Why you were chosen as the presenter. You will want to maximize any advantage you have. This could include knowing the subject matter best or being regarded as the most articulate.
- What you have in common with the audience. You will want to use any means possible to bond with the audience, such as stressing common backgrounds and experiences. You may also refer to people in the audience, particularly those who are well regarded.

2. Consider what you want people to do when you are done, then picture how detailed you will need to be to give them the tools to make the change. Also, contemplate how you can get them to think about the application of your idea. Consider introducing polls from time to time so that you can assess the impact of your ideas and the level of enthusiasm. Polls also demonstrate your interest in the opinions of the audience.

3. Keep it short and simple. Speeches often take longer than planned. Consider that
   - people get bored quickly;
   - the average attention span of most adults is seven minutes;
   - having too many ideas will be confusing.
   Then plan how to keep the message short and to the point.

4. Think about your audience members. Are they looking for inspiration? entertainment? facts? new ideas? a game plan?

5. Plan to incorporate a metaphor or analogy to improve understanding of your key idea.

6. If you intend to use humour, be sure that you are able to do so without hesitation. Tell the joke to as many people as possible in order to test it and improve your ability to deliver the punchline effectively.

7. Consider what you want out of the experience. Do you want to entertain your audience members? Inform them? Teach them new skills? Having clinched the key objective, build your presentation with the appropriate goal and process.

8. Give yourself ample time to prepare. You will be able to collect lots of ideas if you do.

9. As ideas come to mind, write them down in one place.

10. When you craft the speech, put all key ideas on Post-It Notes. Stick them on a wall so that you can see them all. Then
- group like ideas together;
- decide the order of the different ideas.

11. Record key ideas on 3-by-5-inch cue cards. Write key points on each cue card in large, bold letters.

12. Rehearse your speech both in your mind and out loud. Stand up when you do a dry run. Stick your chest out and stand as tall as you can — it will enhance your confidence.

13. Develop a checklist of items you need to take with you or have available.

14. Check out the room in which you will be making the speech. Try to anticipate any problems, such as poor acoustics, and know how you will overcome them.

15. Visualize yourself being very successful. Picture yourself "wowing" the audience.

Speeches

Reducing Stage Fright

$\mathcal{A}$s you progress in your career, you will increasingly be called upon to present ideas to others. And because you will be in the limelight, this is an opportunity for you to shine. But studies indicate that stage fright ranks ahead of death and is the number one fear of North Americans. To help you, here are some tips that will reduce — not eliminate — the anxiety:

1. No matter what you do, don't expect to be without fear — it is normal and good. Some adrenaline rush will improve your awareness and produce an excellent performance.

2. Fear is reduced dramatically by confidence. You can boost your confidence in a number of ways:
- Prepare thoroughly beforehand. Practise your speech as many times as it takes to feel confident about your delivery.
- Make mental preparations. Visualize yourself being successful. Close your eyes and picture yourself knocking the socks off the audience.
- Prepare affirmations. Do some self-talk. Convince yourself that you will be effective, that the audience is interested in what you have to say. Make your affirmations personal. Begin with the "I"

word. Maintain the present tense, such as "I am confident," rather than the future tense, such as "I will be much better."
- Having key points readily available to ensure that you won't lose your train of thought. These key points could be
  - pencilled in on a flip chart just visible enough for you to read but not obvious enough that your audience will see them;
  - highlighted in overheads to give you a structure and a sequence to follow;
  - noted on cue cards that you can follow if you are using a podium.
- Focus on people who are friendly and supportive.

3. Speak only on topics that interest you.

4. As you begin, look for the people who are smiling at you or nodding their support. Imagine that your entire presentation is directed at them.

5. Reduce your anxiety — and the audience's — by starting with something you are familiar with. This will get you into a rhythm and increase your comfort level.

6. Focus on starting off right. Memorize the beginning of your speech so that you start off strongly.

7. Never read your speech. Your pitch will tend to become monotone and the exercise will be more of a reading test than a communication exercise. Consider using cue cards with key ideas written on each. No more than eight to twelve cards are needed for a speech of less than thirty minutes.

Speeches

Enthralling Your Audience

People are spoiled by entertainment on TV and in the movies. Hence, any presentation you make is likely to be to a critical audience whose expectations you cannot control. Here are some things you can do to improve your impact:

1. Start off with a high-impact statement. You may
- challenge the group to use a central concept;
- provide the group with some anecdotal information that sets the scene for what is to come;
- take a poll that will demonstrate the value of the group's investment in time listening to you.

2. Don't read your speech. Picture the entire speech in your head beforehand so that you can imagine the flow of ideas. Then record key ideas on cue cards, each containing a heading and three or four key ideas. Or simply summarize the entire speech on one piece of paper, noting key ideas by highlighting or writing them in bold.

3. Alter your voice modulation often. Speak louder than you normally would, to indicate your confidence.

4. Emphasize key points by:
- pausing before you share them;
- speaking more slowly and deliberately;
- raising your voice;
- punching the air with appropriate hand gestures.

5. Avoid remaining static. Move around from time to time, particularly when you are engaging in dialogue or answering questions. Move closer to the audience to demonstrate your interest.

6. Make the audience think about what you are saying. Ask members questions — even hypothetical ones. Pause to let them contemplate the answers.

7. Poll the audience to show your interest in them and to demonstrate members' support for key points you are proposing.

8. Move constantly to cover different parts of the room. If you sense some hostility, however, focus more on those people who are nodding their agreement with you.

Stress

Too much of a good thing is just right.

MAE WEST

Stress is a fact of modern life. If we don't learn to deal with it, it will deal with us. While we cannot often control the things that cause stress, we can control how we deal with stress. Here are some ways:

1. Don't overreact to things over which you have no control. You can't control turbulence in airplanes, late arrivals by others, or bad behaviour by people's kids. But you can control your reaction to these things. You can drink a glass of wine to calm yourself; you can take deep breaths to regulate your breathing.

2. Leave the situation. Consider leaving the thing that causes the heart palpitations. Go for a walk, go home, or find a place where you feel some solitude, such as the washroom!

3. Take a mental break. Carry an eye-guard with you. Close your door and cover your eyes so that you feel you are in total darkness. Picture yourself in a place where you would be relaxed. Picture yourself on a beach, at home watching your favourite TV show, or any other place that feels calm and comfortable.

4. Take a power nap if you can. A fifteen- or twenty-minute nap will rejuvenate you and charge your batteries, allowing you to cope more effectively with the trials and tribulations around you.

5. Meditate. Close your eyes and try to create a blank slate in your mind. Consider saying the same word over and over in your mind until you achieve a blank state.

6. Take a bath or a shower after a tough day. The warm water will relax you. Linger longer than usual. Use herbal oils or aroma-therapy products to help soothe and relieve the stress from your body and mind.

7. Get a massage. A good masseur will not talk to you but will give you a mental break. He will play music or sounds that will enable your mind to relax and wander.

8. Seek out a confidant. This person will listen without interrupting and will allow you to vent about the things that bother you. He will not offer suggestions either.

9. Be conscious of tension in your body. At your desk, concentrate on each part of your body and work your way up from the tip of your toes to the top of your head. Relax each muscle one at a time.

10. Exercise. Do something that makes you feel good and that forces you to clear your mind of the things that bother you.

11. Put things in perspective. Look at the big picture. Make a mental or physical list of the things you have and for which you should be grateful. Then compare these things with the few things that bother you. You will probably come to the conclusion that you are indeed fortunate.

12. Think about people who have real problems — people who exist from day to day only. Then compare your lot in life and consider how fortunate you are.

13. Avoid artificial means of calming down. Ask your doctor or naturopath about herbal medications such as valerian or St. John's Wort, which are designed to calm. Take as directed.

14. If stress is preventing you from sleeping, consider
- going to bed later;
- drinking herbal teas such as chamomile before bed;
- taking a hot bath to relax;
- never going to bed upset with people — if you are upset, let the person know how you feel, get it off your chest.

15. Stop trying so hard. You may be overdoing things if you
- accept nothing less than perfection;
- need to make every decision;
- fail to delegate;
- don't trust others;
- find yourself working hard without achieving results;
- constantly blame others;
- often get angry;
- allow your emotions to show inappropriately.

Teamwork

Getting Off on the Right Foot

$\mathcal{F}$inding the right combination of people for your team is a critical first step to success. Here are some principles that can act as your guide:

1. Include people who
- have an understanding of the issues;
- have the time or, more realistically, will make the time;
- have the power to make the changes;
- have different perspectives on the problem;
- have quite different personalities, so that they complement each other.

2. Recruit a facilitator. This person will be recruited from a neutral area of your organization. She will run your meetings and help to keep you on track. She typically knows nothing about the technical side of the project, and so can focus her energy on
- ensuring a positive group atmosphere;
- planning and conducting excellent meetings;
- ensuring that the group is on target in meeting its commitments.

3. Restrict membership to between six and twelve members. If you have too few people, members may be swamped with work and fail to meet their commitments. On the other hand, if you have too many people, it will be difficult to develop a sense of cohesiveness and belonging.

4. Get a clear mandate — preferably in writing. The mandate should come from a senior manager and clearly state:
- the problem the team is to tackle;
- whether the team is to
  - make recommendations only;
  - solve the problem;
- the dollars available for discretionary spending;
- any other parameters, such as the team's ability to hire consultants, outsource any business operations, and so on.

5. Develop a plan. Identify
- where you are now;
- where you want to be (the goal);
- what roadblocks will prevent success and how these will be overcome;
- key milestones on the path to ultimate success.

6. Develop a code of conduct. The group members should participate in this exercise and agree on five to ten principles that will guide their conduct towards one another. For example, we agree to
- be open and honest with each other;
- make meetings a priority;
- be supportive of each other;
- meet all commitments undertaken;
- keep discussions within the group in confidence.

Teamwork

Making a Contribution

*M*ost tasks cannot be done in isolation. It takes a number of people, working together, to satisfy internal and external customers. Each person is important, and if anyone fouls up, the entire team and its processes are impacted. Here are some ideas to help your team perform at the highest level:

1. Develop a team mentality. Think "we," not "me."

2. Be open to the ideas of your teammates. No one person has a monopoly on good ideas. Each idea can be built on until it becomes viable. In fact, the greater the contribution by all team members, the higher the chances of a successful implementation, as buy-in will be assured.

3. Be respectful of others. Listen to their ideas. Don't cut them off. Listen to be influenced. Think about why you should be influenced rather than why the idea won't work.

4. Be approachable. When people come to you, project openness through your voice and body language. Smile. Lean forward.

Maintain eye contact. Ask open-ended questions. Also, thank people for sharing their ideas with you.

5. Be helpful. Offer assistance when you see others being overwhelmed with work or unable to solve a problem. Chances are you will build up goodwill that you can draw on when you are under the gun.

6. Be a role model. Behave the way you expect others to behave. But have minimal expectations that others will follow. If they do — great; if they don't, simply feel good about your role.

7. Accept others as they are. You can't change people. You can change only your behaviour towards them.

8. Avoid rewarding people for things they do that annoy you. Laughing at stupidity at team meetings, for example, will simply serve to encourage the dysfunctional behaviour. However, if the person does something you appreciate, let him know.

9. Celebrate your team's achievements. This will encourage cohesiveness and pride in what you are doing. For example, if your team has reached a new plateau in its performance, bring baked goods to your next meeting.

10. Avoid territorialism. Too much pride in a team can lead to counterproductive behaviour that undermines other teams. Your loyalty is first to your organization and second to your team, not the other way around.

11. Play a positive role at team meetings. The meetings are a great opportunity to communicate, solve problems, develop plans, and

make decisions. They are important for the effective running of the team. You will make the meetings more effective if you

- volunteer for a role at the meeting, such as secretary, recorder, or timekeeper;
- stick to the topic;
- avoid interrupting others;
- avoid dominating the discussion;
- encourage others to share their ideas;
- avoid repeating ideas;
- volunteer for action items.

12. Share information readily. In fact, over-communicate — people should never be able to accuse you of hiding or withholding information.

13. Let people know if you're not happy. Don't sweep issues under the carpet. Deal with issues professionally, so as not to make more or bigger problems than actually exist.

14. When dealing with problems, avoid finger-pointing. Instead, deal with the issue assertively. This requires that you:

- Make the problem yours. Use the "I" word rather than the "you" word.
- Let people know how you feel. For example, start off by saying "I'm really angry when this or that happens."
- Get agreement to the way you feel. Say, "Can you see why I'm upset?"
- Ask others who are involved how they can help you solve the problem. You should never tell them what to do, since you will "own" the solution and they will not.
- Listen to their solutions and then thank them for helping you.

15. If you are not sure where the team is headed, create your own vision. Share it with others, particularly your leader. Determine how valid your vision really is.

16. Train others. While being a specialist adds to your value on the team, it also makes the team vulnerable if you are away or transferred. Offer to teach others your skills.

17. Learn other jobs. You can increase your value by being able to take over for others who are away. Don't make people feel threatened by demanding that they show you what they do. Simply offer to help if they intend to be away, so they won't be overloaded on their return.

Teamwork

Dealing with Difficult People

$\mathcal{L}$ife is full of challenges, but few are as difficult as having to work closely with people whose behaviour exceeds what you consider acceptable. Since these people could impact your worklife significantly, here are some ideas that can help:

1. In general, follow the philosophy of the Serenity Prayer. The prayer goes like this:

> *God grant me the serenity to accept the*
> *things I cannot change*
> *The courage to change the things I can*
> *And the wisdom to know the difference.*

Translated, this philosophy suggests that you should accept people for what they are, since you cannot change their personalities. However, you can change some things. You can:
- let difficult people know how their actions affect you;
- avoid them;
- ignore them;
- ask them to stop doing things that impact you without commenting on their personalities or attitudes;

- let them know when they have done something that pleases you;
- act as a model for how you want them to behave.

2. In meetings you can:
   - Prevent difficult people from dominating by asking the facilitator if there are other opinions.
   - Offer to write all ideas on the flip chart. This will demonstrate that there are a variety of ideas, each of which is equally valid.
   - Ask them to substantiate their opinions with facts. Say, "Could you give some examples of when that happened?" or "How many times has that happened?"
   - Counter their exaggerations with data and evidence of your own.
   - Let them know that their opinions are held by the minority of team members by canvassing other opinions. Then say, "Gee, I respect your opinion, but it seems that you are the only one with that opinion."
   - Ask that frivolous and unrelated ideas be dealt with later or off-line.
   - Ask for examples of the kind of issues brought up, so as to expose that the statement is an opinion and not a fact.
   - Be assertive. If you have a strong opinion that is different, speak slowly and deliberately, raising your voice to emphasize key points. Also, lean forward and maintain eye contact to demonstrate confidence in your opinion.

Teamwork

No man stands so tall as when he stoops to help a boy.

ANONYMOUS

Most people are either extroverts or introverts. Extroverts tend to be more outspoken and usually think aloud. They talk before they think. Introverts think before they talk. Sometimes, they think so much that they don't talk at all. But thinking often enables introverts to have wonderful ideas. It would be a tragedy if no one canvassed the idea from these less talkative people. Here's how to draw introverts out:

IN MEETINGS

1. • Give introverts time to think. Let them know ahead of time what issues will be raised at the meeting.
   • Give people a chance to write their ideas down before they call them out. This will give the introverts time to think.
   • Suggest a round robin. Say, "Let's go around the table to give everyone a chance. If people don't have an idea, they can say 'pass.'"
   • Watch the body language of the introvert. While introverts are typically more difficult to read, they sometimes give a clue that

they have an idea. Their mouths begin to open, their eyes light up, or they lean forward. If you suspect that they have specific ideas, ask them for their thoughts.

- Suggest making the introvert the recorder. By standing up, the introvert will be more likely to interact with the group.

OUTSIDE MEETINGS

2.
- Approach the introvert for ideas. Plant the seed by describing your problem. Then approach him later to find out what he thinks.
- Value her ideas anytime they are volunteered by thanking her — regardless of whether you like her idea.

Time Management

To realize the value of one year:
Ask a student who has failed a final exam.
To realize the value of one month:
Ask a mother who has just given birth to a premature baby.
To realize the value of one hour:
Ask the lovers who are waiting to meet.
To realize the value of one minute:
Ask the person who missed the plane, train or bus.
To realize the value of one millisecond:
Ask the person who has won a silver medal in the Olympics.
Time waits for no one.

UNKNOWN

*T*ime is impossible to manage. We cannot change time. There are always seven days in a week, twenty-four hours in a day, sixty minutes in an hour, and sixty seconds in a minute. What we can do is use our time effectively so that we succeed in our professional and personal lives. Here are some ideas to help:

1. Prioritize your activities. Always do things that will maintain and enhance your reputation with your customer/client.

2. Each day create a "to do" list. Estimate how long each item will take. Do not try to do things that will give you no flexibility to deal with unforeseen matters that arise each day. Items that will take you beyond 60 percent of available time should be put on your list for another day.

3. Rank all items on your "to do" list for importance. Things to do with internal and external clients should be given A ratings; personal business activities get a B; frivolous and fun items get a C.

4. Do one thing at a time. Focus on completing the task so that you can move on to the next with a clear head. Increase your energy as the task nears completion so you can get it out of the way.

5. Reduce the clutter on your desk so your mind can focus on the task ahead. This can be achieved by:
- Handling each thing that comes across your desk just once. Make a decision with each item — do it, file it, or dump it.
- Working on one task at a time.
- Recording information only if there is a good chance you will refer to it later.
- Getting yourself a large wastepaper basket and using it a lot! We often clutter our desks with stuff we never use. So take courage and file more stuff away permanently.

6. Use every minute of time to get things done, so you have as much free time as possible to relax and think. Here are some ways to improve your productivity:
- Use a cellular phone to return calls during travel time.

- Make better use of public transit. While sitting on the bus or train, you can
  - go through your mail;
  - work on your laptop and respond to e-mails;
  - prepare for meetings;
  - plan presentations;
  - sit back and take a mental look at your effectiveness;
  - read articles you have been carrying around.
- Keep articles that will promote your professional development. Read them when you are in line-ups, waiting for meetings to start and at other down times.
- Try to locate yourself as close as possible to people you work with. This will save travel time, including time walking to and from their offices.
- Avoid telephone tag by leaving detailed messages for people you can't get hold of. Also, if you have voice mail, ask people to leave you detailed messages.
- Do two things at once, when appropriate. Examples of multi-tasking are
  - reading while exercising;
  - watching a video while exercising;
  - listening to tapes while travelling.

7. Reduce the time you spend in meetings:
   - Get there on time. Thanks to your example, others might be encouraged to follow your lead to ensure that meetings start promptly.
   - Ask your colleagues to agree to start meetings on time whether people are there or not. This will reward punctuality, not tardiness.
   - Ask the chairperson when the meeting will end. This will increase people's consciousness of being on time.

- Ask if you can be excused when items that don't pertain to you are being dealt with.
- Offer to be a timekeeper. Alert the participants when they are running over time on any agenda items.

8. Deal effectively with time-wasters. Don't engage in idle chat with people who have too much time on their hands. When you see them coming:
   - Avoid making eye contact with them. They may then go on to someone else who is interested and will make the time.
   - Stand up when they approach. This will discourage them from sitting, getting comfortable, and taking more of your valuable time than you would like.
   - Close your door when you urgently need to finish a task and require the additional quiet to be able to concentrate.
   - If you have an assistant, ask him to guard your door. Give him permission to prevent people from walking in when your door is closed.
   - Establish a quiet time with co-workers. This hour a day will allow you to do the many things that would otherwise clutter your mind and prevent you from communicating effectively with your fellow associates.

9. Greet and meet people outside your office. In this way, you increase control of the situation to terminate any discussion when you feel it is appropriate.

10. Remove chairs near your desk. This will prevent people from sitting down for idle chatter.

11. If people approach you asking for a minute of your time, either say no, letting them know that this is not a good time, or say,

"Well, I actually have three minutes." Then look at your watch, so people are conscious of the fact that their time with you is being monitored.

12. If your organization has a "flex time" policy, use it either to get in earlier than the traditional start of business or to stay a little later. In this way, you will have time to get things done without constant interruptions.

13. Change the layout of your furniture. You can create more time by doing the following:
- Moving your desk out of a high-traffic area that encourages people to stop and chat.
- Moving closer to people you work with so as to reduce travel time.
- Positioning your desk in a way that does not enable people to see your face. This way, you will have fewer people bothering you.
- Getting the best chair your company can afford. A good chair will give your back additional support to enable you to work longer without feeling pain and muscle strain.

14. Remain as alert as possible. You will increase your concentration and work speed if you
- take frequent stretch breaks;
- exercise;
- take short mental breaks to clear your mind.

15. Invest in a time-management system. This could be a paper-based system or the appropriate software for your computer. Hallmarks of an effective paper-based system are
- a separate daily "to do" list section, which allows you to insert tasks for future days;

- a calendar section for all your appointments;
- a section for all your key contacts.

16. Effective software will include
- a task list that will appear as a reminder on your screen when something needs to be done;
- the ability to review the schedules of your associates and book meeting times;
- a calendar with reminder features;
- integrated e-mailing capabilities that enable you to find a person and, with one click of a mouse, immediately create an e-mail template.

Training

Getting the Most Out of Workshops

Every blade of grass has its Angel that bends over and whispers, "Grow, grow."

THE TALMUD

There are four levels by which workshops are evaluated:

- Level 1 — Did participants enjoy the experience?
- Level 2 — Did participants learn?
- Level 3 — Did participants use the skills?
- Level 4 — Did participants' performance improve?

Clearly, Levels 1 and 2 happen in the workshop and contribute to Levels 3 and 4. If Levels 3 and 4 are not reached, the training is largely a waste of time and money. Here are some ideas to avoid such waste.

1. Evaluate whether you really need to go to a workshop at all. Can you get the information you need from:

- a colleague?
- a book (self-help)?
- an Internet search?
- your manager?
- self-paced computer-based training?

2. If the skill is best acquired in a workshop format, find out if this is available internally or externally. The advantages of an in-house workshop include:

- Learning the same skill as others in a similar situation. This will give a critical mass of people a better chance of using new techniques. No one person will feel like an oddball trying new things on his own.
- Having the ability to network and share successes and problems with others who are easily accessible.
- Less time-wasting. The workshop will probably be tailored so participants can deal with real issues.
- Case studies will be confined to organizational issues.
- The program may be just in time and scheduled right before you need to put the new skills into practice.

3. The advantages of an outside workshop include:

- The ability to stand back and see the big picture. The workshop cannot deal with the nitty-gritty issues you face. Rather, it would take more of a global approach.
- Networking opportunities. Sometimes we believe our organization to be unique. By meeting people from a variety of organizations, we often find that we have similar issues. And more important, we may discover new innovative solutions that have application in our organization.

4. During a workshop, be it internal or off-site, you will improve your learning if you:

- Let the instructor know if you have specific issues you would like to have addressed.
- Familiarize yourself with the course objectives. Highlight the ones of greatest importance to you. Focus on them.
- Write down key ideas constantly. Develop a summary daily.

- Ask lots of questions. If you feel that some of your questions are off track or of little interest to others, corner the trainer at breaks or at the end of the day, to ensure that you get answers.
- Participate with enthusiasm.
- Practise skills at every opportunity. Participate in role-playing rather than acting as observer.
- Sit closer to the front to ensure fewer distractions.
- Ask for feedback from the instructor and fellow participants on how you are doing, particularly when you're involved in a role play. Pay close attention to what you are told, without being defensive.
- Stretch yourself. The workshop is an opportunity to try things that you've never done before. Failure and mistakes can be an effective part of the learning process.
- Ask for feedback on your effectiveness. Listen without being defensive. Make notes on how you can improve.
- Find someone you trust so you can mentor and support each other after the workshop.
- Offer to give your boss or peers a summary of what you gained at the workshop. This will present you with the great challenge of getting your head around the key concepts.

5. Before you attend a workshop, consider these issues:
   - What is your preferred learning style? Do you, for example, prefer to listen and observe rather than do things experientially? What process will predominate at the workshop? Some, particularly the one-day-wonder seminars, appeal to the observers but have little value for the hands-on learner.
   - Who is providing the workshop? What are his or her credentials? What is his or her training style? Does it match your learning style?
   - How effective was the workshop for others?

Training

With Peers

If you want to be prosperous for a year, grow grain;
If you want to be prosperous for ten years, grow trees;
If you want to be prosperous for a lifetime, grow people.

PROVERB

The best interests of an organization are served by people who are multi-skilled. These people fill in for people who are away temporarily or overloaded. So while it enhances your power to be a specialist, the sole provider of a niche skill or technology, it's in your organization's interest to have others who are able to do your job, to at least an 80 percent competency level. If you're asked to train someone to do your job, here's how you should go about doing so:

1. Before the training, meet with your fellow employee to establish:
- Her level of enthusiasm for the task at hand.
- How much she knows about the task. Ask:
  - Has she ever done this before?
  - Has she done something similar?
- What similar knowledge and skills she possess.
- Any barriers that will inhibit her learning, such as language or dexterity.

2. Ask if he has any concerns about doing the task. Try to alleviate his concerns by describing how you will help overcome them.

3. Try to establish how she likes to learn. Is she:
   - Auditory? These people learn best by listening.
   - Visual? These people learn best by seeing a demonstration.
   - Kinesthetic? These people like to learn something by doing it.

   While a person may have a favourite style of learning — one you should focus on — it is best to cover all three for maximum impact.

4. Document the process as you know it. If it is complex, break it down into "bite-sized" pieces. Whenever possible, provide diagrams and drawings; after all, a picture is worth a thousand words.

5. Document the standards of performance so that the trainee will know what constitutes an acceptable performance.

6. Set a date, place, and time for the training. Plan to do it near the time when he will need to use his new skills.

7. Meet with the trainee for the transfer of information. Make her feel comfortable by
   - assuring her that you will work at her pace;
   - letting her know that you are confident of her ability;
   - encouraging her to ask as many questions as she needs to.

8. Confirm the purpose of the training. Let the trainee know how many sessions you will have and what help he can expect from you.

9. Explain how the task fits into the overall process of the particular product or service being provided.

10. Explain the goal of your training and your expectations in terms of the standards that should be achieved.

11. Demonstrate the task. If it large and complex, break the task down and demonstrate one part at a time.

12. Monitor the reaction of the trainee. What is her body language telling you? Is she smiling, acknowledging understanding, and showing interest? Respond to any negativity by identifying and dealing with the issue.

13. Let the trainee try the task. Stand back and observe. Be careful not to intervene too quickly if he makes a mistake; wait a little while to see if he will correct himself.

14. Observe her body language. Saying that she understands may be true or it may be a polite way of not wanting to admit a lack of understanding. You will generally know that she understands if
- her eyes are focused;
- she is nodding;
- she shows some impatience to try it herself;
- she is paraphrasing your explanation.

15. Ask him if he can do it. If so, let him try. If not, show him again.

16. Give praise at any sign of progress. The greater the progress, the bigger your praise should be.

17. With each step mastered, go on to the next step until the process is complete.

18. Have her document your instructions in her own words. This "template" will enable her to do the job without having to check with you when she runs into difficulties.

19. Finish the training with a symbolic celebration. Congratulate the learner. Assure him of your support. Invite him to call on you if he encounters any difficulties in the future.

Vision

Establishing Your Own

$\mathcal{J}$t is fashionable for organizations to be guided by a vision, usually that of the CEO. Why? Well, it provides a direction, clarity of purpose, and focus for actions. The same should apply to you personally. However, your personal vision would be even more motivation because you created it. You own it, so it will motivate your actions and drive you to success. Here's how you can create your own vision:

1. Get some crayons — multi-coloured Crayola crayons are wonderful — then get a clean sheet of paper. Next, imagine yourself as a child of perhaps three or four. Imagine through that child's eyes what you will look like when you are most successful. Draw that picture and do it quickly. Do not think too much — adult behaviour will inhibit your creativity. Let your hand and the crayons do the talking.

2. Stop after three to four minutes. You don't need to compete with Rembrandt!

3. Reflect on your picture. What key themes do you see? A sun for optimism? A mountain for climbing to achievement? A big house or money to depict success?

4. Write, in one or two sentences, clear thoughts on what you aspire to be.

5. Remember your vision, the Super Me. Use it to drive you, motivate you, and change your behaviour. When in difficulty, imagine how the Super Me would handle the situation.

6. On a daily basis, begin to act the Super Me. Behaving as if you are already successful will make you feel good and appear exceptional to those around you.

7. Make a list of obstacles that are preventing you from achieving the Super Me. Eliminate items you cannot control. Divide the remaining items into short- (one year), medium- (two to five years), and long-term projects (five+ years). Forget the long-term items — they are too distant. Focus on the short-term items. Space them out so that you don't drown in trying to do them all at once.

8. Post your current short-term goal where you can see it every day. Perhaps put a Post-It Note on your bathroom mirror. When it has been achieved, celebrate by treating yourself to something special. Then post the next goal. Remember: "The journey of a thousand miles must begin with a single step."

Voice Mail

Communicating is the number-one way of getting things done. With all our modern systems, we are communicating more often, but not necessarily more successfully. Voice-mail systems are everywhere. Unfortunately, their introduction to organizations is hindering rather than improving communications. Here is how you can make more efficient use of this communications tool:

1. When setting up your voice-mail message, consider these ideas:
- Make your message pleasant and welcoming.
- Record a message of no longer than fifteen seconds. In that time, you should state
  - your name;
  - where you are (i.e., "away from my desk," "on holiday," "at a conference");
  - that the person leave his name, phone number, and a complete message;
  - how long it may take to get back to the caller;
  - your appreciation for the call.
- Do not record your message using a speaker phone. It will make you sound as if you're on another planet.

- Listen to your message to ensure that it sends a tone of friendliness and professionalism. If it doesn't, record it until you are satisfied that it does.

2. When calling someone who has voice mail, leave
   - your name;
   - your phone number;
   - the reason for your call;
   - a time when you can be reached.

   In this way, you will have started the communication. If the person calls back when you're not there, he or she can then close the loop by leaving a message for you.

3. If you are leaving important details, speak more slowly and deliberately, imagining the other party making notes while you speak.

4. Avoid leaving personal and confidential information on voice mail.

Working at Home

I work as hard as anyone, and I get so little done.
I'd do so much you'd be surprised,
if I could just get organized.

DOUGLAS MALLOCH

In a drive to reduce costs and take advantage of the ease of electronic communications, organizations are becoming increasingly partial to having people work at home. For most people, this is a whole new experience — one that requires discipline and focus. Here are some ideas that can enhance the experience.

1. Contract with your family not to disturb you during certain hours. This will help you increase your motivation to work.

2. Locate your office far from high-traffic areas so that you won't see or hear people. The basement or the end of a hallway is preferable.

3. Keep your door closed to avoid disruptions. Post a Do Not Disturb sign on the door.

4. Reduce the initial sense of isolation by going out during lunch. Go to a mall so that you feel you are part of the wider world.

5. Avoid taking on additional daytime chores that were not previously your responsibility. Alternatively, do these chores in the time you once spent commuting, at either the beginning or the end of the day.

6. Set goals for yourself each day. Focus on completing at least one meaningful task every day. Reward yourself with a cookie or some other token benefit.

7. Don't isolate yourself totally from your peers at work. Attend office meetings at least once every two weeks. There is no substitute for face-to-face communication.

8. Communicate with peers who have made the same transition as you. Find out how they are doing and learn if they have particular strategies that helped make the transition successful.

9. Furnish your work area to make it look and feel just as it did in your old office.

10. Don't fall prey to the temptation to stay in your pajamas — you will be inclined to act sloppy.

11. Maintain a routine that requires you to work certain hours, start at a certain time and finish at a certain time. Also, pause mid-morning and -afternoon to refresh, stretch and take a mental break.

Writing Skills

Our life is frittered away by detail . . . Simplify, simplify.

HENRY DAVID THOREAU

$\mathscr{I}$n business, as in life, first impressions are very important. Often, your first contact with clients will be written — through letters, brochures, sales kits, annual reports, and so on. Here are some basic guidelines that will help you improve your writing skills and present yourself as a competent, articulate, knowledgeable professional.

1. Be clear and concise. Make sure your writing is free of jargon, nonessential words, and unnecessarily complicated sentences.

2. Never use five words where one will do. For example, instead of "at the present time," simply use "now"; rather than "due to the fact that," write "because."

3. Favour simple words over complicated words. Don't write "utilize" if "use" will do.

4. Be authoritative — this gives people confidence in your abilities. Ruthlessly prune your writing of qualifiers — "a bit," "kind of," "quite," "very" — that weaken your persuasiveness. A sentence such as "This is quite a good product, and I'm pretty sure you will like it" can be deadly.

5. Opt for the active voice over the passive. "He hit the ball over the left-field fence" is preferable to "The ball was hit by him over the left-field fence."

6. Never lie or make exaggerated claims in your writing. If your reader catches you in even one small lie, everything in your report or letter becomes suspect.

7. Keep your writing accessible and appealing. Use anecdotes, sub-heads, sidebars, bullets, and graphics where appropriate. Write in a style that is conversational and friendly, but don't be careless or resort to slang.

The easiest way to improve your writing is to learn to edit yourself. Read over any written work, even if it's just a one-page letter, and prune any superfluous words or examples, any passive constructions, any unnecessary jargon. More than anything else, you must be clear in your mind about what it is you wish to communicate. Remember: a cluttered mind produces cluttered writing.

When you're writing, it's a good idea to have a guide to punctuation handy, as well as those other tools for good writing, a dictionary and a thesaurus. Don't rely too heavily on the programs built into your word-processing software.